"*Neighborhood Transformation* is a telling testimony to the power of religion in building and fostering community among immigrants in the US. It offers rich theological insights for appropriating the theme of hospitality for building a community of strangers in a pluralistic world. I highly recommend the book for students and scholars of theology, immigration studies, cultural studies, and African studies."

—**Akintunde E. Akinade**, professor of theology, Georgetown University

"In a fast-moving prose, Olusegun Osineye lays out a fascinating practical theology of church and society. In deft precise movements, the analysis of church and society relations reconstitutes itself into a provocative public theology of undocumented immigrants in the United States. This is an excellent resource book for ministers and scholars who are after God's heart for immigrants or strangers in the world."

—**Nimi Wariboko**, author of *Transcripts of the Sacred in Nigeria: Beautiful, Monstrous, Ridiculous*

"I highly recommend this work. Olusegun Osineye takes you beyond the complexities and controversies of immigration into a world of compassion, laced with duty of care and Jesus-like empathy towards undocumented African migrants in the US."

—**Victor Jatula**, assistant professor of press and politics, Brunel University London

"This book is a must-read for all pastors and church leaders, documented and undocumented immigrants. The work creates a platform for continued efforts to sooth the pains of many hardworking undocumented immigrants striving for survival in a difficult environment. Undocumented persons face discrimination due to their origin, language, and socio-economic handicaps. However, when the playing field is more favorable, most of them become assets, not liabilities to the country. Kudos to Olusegun Osineye for a job well done."

—**Dokun Adewunmi**, rector/missioner, All Saints Anglican Church

"My take on this book after reading it is this: It is a must-read by all immigrants, young and old, legal or in the process of becoming legal residents. Take advantage of the economic opportunities that the USA represents which is line with the Word of God Most High to the immigrants in Jeremiah 29:4-7."

—'**Bunmi Akindebe**, senior pastor, Salem Gospel Mission Int'l

Neighborhood Transformation

Neighborhood Transformation

A Specialized Ministry to African Immigrants

Olusegun Solomon Osineye

FOREWORD BY
Jacob K. Olupona

RESOURCE *Publications* · Eugene, Oregon

NEIGHBORHOOD TRANSFORMATION
A Specialized Ministry to African Immigrants

Resource Publications
An Imprint of Wipf and Stock Publishers
199 W. 8th Ave., Suite 3
Eugene, OR 97401

www.wipfandstock.com

PAPERBACK ISBN: 978-1-6667-8892-1
HARDCOVER ISBN: 978-1-6667-8893-8
EBOOK ISBN: 978-1-6667-8894-5

VERSION NUMBER 07/24/24

Contents

Foreword

Olusegun Solomon Osineye's first book, *Neighborhood Transformation: A Specialized Ministry to African Immigrants*, is a fascinating account of how undocumented African immigrants in New England are drawing on their deep faith to transform their neighborhoods. Osineye reaffirms and reimagines the purpose of the Christian church through the lens of undocumented African immigrants in New England. He asks how the good news preached in the gospel calls the church and fellow Christians to serve those African immigrants who are denied the fundamental rights of citizens in the United States. This case allows Osineye to put on full display his dedication to ministry and theological rallying cry for a more just world. Osineye's inspiring words cement his position as an up-and-coming clergyman and scholar in the pursuit of a Christian church that lives up to the moral mandates and ethical lessons of the Bible.

Osineye's research is as theoretical as it is practical. He not only offers well-thought-out philosophical and theological theories about the purpose of church, he also carefully analyzes how undocumented African immigrants navigate a lack of resources. Based on this spiritual framework and on-site research, he outlines how faith communities and local governments can provide immigrants the necessary resources to flourish in their new communities. I am particularly impressed with how Osineye engages central questions pertaining to diasporic faith communities, such as religion, immigration, pluralistic societies, and the law. This manuscript is a significant contribution to the fields of religion and diaspora studies.

As an emerging scholar, Osineye critically analyzes the ideas and theories of the social gospel movement to conceptualize a "church without walls." This idea is a powerful theological position from which Osineye proposes a supportive and present form of ministry for and with undocumented African immigrants in New England. Osineye sees this ministry as the vehicle toward neighborhood transformation, the work's moral vision for a thriving faith community in the diaspora. In conclusion, the book in my opinion succeeds in raising important conceptual and substantive matters as they relate to the invisible religious communities he has labelled the undocumented who are too often left behind. It proves beyond any reasonable doubt that, given the physical and emotional abuse that these groups of people suffer, the church has a moral and theological responsibility to provide a strong spiritual response to ameliorate their longtime suffering and neglect in the society and the diaspora.

Jacob K. Olupona N.N.OM; FNAL

Harvard University

Professor of African and African American Studies,
Faculty of Arts and Sciences

Chair of African and African American Studies,
Faculty of Arts and Sciences

Professor of African Religious Traditions,
Harvard Divinity School

Introduction

The Purpose of the Church

WHAT EXACTLY IS THE purpose of the church? How do Christians know if the church is living up to the authenticity of its calling? Regarding the marks of a true church, what is it that when we see it, we can boldly affirm, "This is it! This is what I expect the church to look like!"

Although theologians identify several historical marks of a true church, those are not my preoccupation at this time. I am only concerned about the church living out its real purpose as exemplified by Jesus in Matthew 25:35–40. But the question is, what does that purpose look like? How would I know if I have genuinely found it and engaged in its practice? I find myself asking why people still resist the gospel, with its inherent promise of "good news." What exactly is going on with the church, especially with the social dysfunction that encompasses us? How should we think about the real purpose of the church? What procedures or processes do we need to embrace for the church to live out its real purpose? What is the generalized conceptual understanding of the notion called the "church," and what interpretation do we want to give it in this contemporary time?

In my estimation, the church is not where we carry out some good and noble activities for religiosity's sake. The church is that sacred space of being, where it is expected to live out purposefully according to the true meaning of her creed—to feed the hungry, clothe the naked, shelter the homeless, visit the sick and help strangers.[1] These are the ministry practices in which I believe the contemporary church should be involved.

The general outline of this book is divided into six chapters, beginning with an introduction. The introductory section focuses on how to fulfill the purpose of the church, while the conclusion at the end after the sixth chapter deals with the vocation of African immigrants. Chapter 1 aims at exposing the challenges that undocumented African immigrants (uDAIs) face in the U.S.A. The chapter will also tackle the lack of resources that hinders their flourishing. Finally, it will suggest the required steps needed to provide emotional, legal, and spiritual support for uDAIs in New England.[2]

Chapter 2 deals with the changing contexts for ministry and the inspiration I received through the social gospel movement. During my five years of theological graduate study, I have seen how my firmly held theological beliefs have been shaken to their foundation. The result of this is the tension that now exists between my previous conception of the faith community and the challenges of building a contemporary one with emerging new contexts. Based on this, I have been forced to reconceptualize the notion of "church without walls."

Chapter 3 will describe my theological and biblical vision for neighborhood transformation. The notion of neighborhood transformation has become the ideal way for me to extend the church's true purpose in the community to which I belong through a specialized ministry to the uDAIs in New England.

---

1. Matt 25:35–40.

2. uDAIs is an acronym of undocumented African immigrants. The first letter u is written in the lower case to denote the fact that undocumented immigrants are not supposed to be accorded the basic rights and privileges of a normal citizen. Hence, the uppercase D emphasizes the rights and privileges that the undocumented are lacking as individuals.

I will begin the chapter with my vision of neighborhood transformation. Then I will conclude with what I consider to be my vision of the connection between the New Jerusalem and the African immigrant neighborhood.

Chapter 4 will dwell on the philosophical framework of community building. The approach will be to dissect the concept of community before contextualizing it within the context of the Christian calling to build a community of strangers in a pluralistic society such as the United States of America.

Chapter 5 will examine the theology of hospitality. Subsequently, an effort will be made to focus on one of the core principles of community formation through congregational hospitality practices. The chapter will discuss the biblical basis for hospitality as a model approach for treating strangers, citing relevant examples from the Hebrew Bible. The chapter will also look at the perils and shortcomings of the Old Testament practice of hospitality. Furthermore, it will modify the concept of the Old Testament hospitality to align it with modern practices of a contemporary theology of hospitality. The chapter will do a little bit of exegesis of scriptures about hospitality in the entire Bible, followed by the treatment of some sermon and Bible study topics for a robust understanding of the subject matter.

Chapter 6 aims to design a legitimate incarnational ministry that provides resources and support to uDAIs in New England. Therefore, the chapter will describe a specialized outreach program called Justice for Jeshurun Immigration Ministry (JJIM), a model patterned after the National Justice for Our Neighbors (NJFON), a ministry intended to serve uDAIs. I will discuss the transformational leadership practice of Ronald Heifetz's adaptive leadership theory to address the varied immigration cases that African immigrants will bring to our attention needing solutions. I will also examine some of the future goals that I hope to pursue by utilizing the idea of Robert Quinn in his book *Deep Change: Discovering the Leader Within*. Initiating an immigration ministry like JJIM will require a profound change—a significant departure from the norms or the familiar in existing models of immigration outreach. Quinn envisaged that for a deep change to occur, the leader must confront the undiscussable that threatens any community's continued existence.[3] One of the national issues that seem mostly undiscussable today is the immigration issue. My church will want to be part of those who create a regular conversation around the immigration crisis confronting us as a nation.

The conclusion will focus on the vocation of African immigrants. My church's mission is expected to be more than just feeding the hungry and clothing the naked. The aim here is to motivate and compel African immigrants in the U.S. to focus on give-back programs that will touch people's lives in their specific homelands in Africa.

3. Quinn, *Deep Change*, 148–89.

Chapter 1

Everyday Challenges of Undocumented African Immigrants

A MIDDLE-AGED UDAI WHOM I will name Jessica (real name re-dacted) brought a proposal to me to write an affidavit on her behalf and that of her "arranged husband." The man was only pretending to be her real husband in the eyes of the law, and they mutually consented to have no sexual intimacy in their relationship. She wanted me to write that I had known them to be husband and wife, publicly displaying their affection, since she started attending our church in Everett, Massachusetts, in May 2019. She also wanted me to take photographs with them in my full priestly regalia to submit to the United States Citizenship and Immigration Services (USCIS) office to prove their relationship and connection to our church family. I did not wish to lie and to drag my divine calling through the mud of unethical pastoral boundary shifting. But her plea created a real dilemma. The plight and the hardship that she and other undocumented immigrants face are real, but her pro-posal to escape the situation contradicted my calling.

In another dilemma reflecting everyday situations among African immigrants, Johnson (real name redacted) is a young college graduate from Nigeria. He has unpaid tuition fees, is jobless, has unstable housing and pressure from family and friends to send money back home to Nigeria. Further, he has a challenge trying to convince his soon-to-be in-laws that he is not an opportunist. My wife invited him to our house for fellowship about three years ago, and over the first four months of our interactions, Johnson shared his challenging stories. When Johnson joined our church, he was very active, in the sense that he was always willing to run errands for the church leadership. On one occasion, he drove me around the Malden area to look for a possible church venue where our growing church could meet and worship.

After much prayer and pastoral support, Johnson found employment in a high-paying company. Perhaps benefitting from my spiritual support and counsel, he also started getting along with his soon-to-be in-laws. Unfortunately, tragedy struck again! Johnson was made redundant, barely two months into the job, because of a takeover by another company. This only became known to me after persistent inquiries from my wife and me. At this time, Johnson became very resentful toward us, refusing to accept our phone calls and not responding to our text messages. He requested that he be left alone for some time, because according to him, as the situation stood, he believed that we did not have the resources to help him solve his challenges. He was partially correct. Our young and upcoming church could not resolve Johnson's practical needs at that time. The reason was because Johnson confronted with several issues: second job loss, the fear of losing his F1 visa status, a possible relationship breakup with his fiancée, and potential homelessness.

The two cases mentioned above are realities shared by other immigrants in the African church communities. Many African immigrant churches do not want to confront undocumented immigration challenges systematically, so they pretend to be blind, as did the priest and Levite in the Parable of the Good Samaritan.[1]

1. Luke 10:29–35.

They pass by on the side of the road rather than assist the stranded man who could no longer help himself. This attitude is similar to the one noted by Rev. Henry Maxwell, a fictional character in Charles Sheldon's book *In His Steps*, wherein the affluent congregation of Raymond's first church displayed when he saw the shabby-looking young man who visited their church uninvited. The young man had been jobless for ten months. Finding another job had been impossible, primarily because of a lack of sensitivity from the many so-called Christian people within the neighborhood. They ignored the man and pretended that his problem was not their concern, let alone a critical priority. Avoiding responsibility, they claimed that they were not the architects of his misfortune.[2] But avoiding immigrants does not take the question away: what can the African churches do for uDAIs?

What Is Going On?—The Problem in Perspective

This book is written to tackle the lack of resources and provide emotional, legal, and spiritual support for many undocumented African immigrants in New England. The problem has been exacerbated by the systemic marginalization of uDAIs as a voiceless minority group in a pluralistic society like the U.S., perhaps due to a lack of self-awareness of what resources are available for them and lack of effective coordination of African immigrants by most of the first-generation African churches in the U.S.[3]

Undocumented immigrants cannot access potential resources because immigration services, especially legal advice, are costly. But the good news here in New England is that there are attorneys who often agree to work pro bono. However, the unfortunate thing about this is that many uDAIs do not know about these free legal services. Another obstacle is that many

2. Sheldon, *In His Steps*, 8–16.

3. African churches referred to here are the first-generation African churches in the U.S. from 1980 onward. It does not consist of all the African America churches in the U.S. since the time of the slave trade.

undocumented immigrants are often unwilling to share their stories with untrusted legal representatives for fear of being exposed to sudden deportation. I experienced this in my casual interaction with some of the uDAIs. The majority of them declined to participate in the discussion of the subject matter for fear of sudden exposure to law enforcement agencies.

Despite this challenge, I was determined to find a way around the problem to bring respite to the suffering of many African immigrants whose cases of survival are even more precarious than the real-life cases mentioned at the beginning of this book. My solemn resolution was to get to meet them right in the neighborhood and locate where their shoes are pinching and provide transformative help for them.

Transformation through Design Thinking

My focus is on human transformation by becoming involved in the neighborhood, where God says he is now resident according to Revelation 21:3: ". . . God has moved into the neighborhood, making his home with men and women! They are his people, he is their God" (MSG). To carry out my neighborhood transformation, I will utilize a transformation concept called "design thinking," which is simply the performance of a series of thought experiments to identify the best possible solution to the issue at hand.[4] According to Linda Bergquist and Allan Karr, there are three church renewal approaches in their book *Church Turned Inside Out: A Guide for Designers, Refiners, and Re-Aligners*. The three church renewal approaches are re-designing, refining, and re-aligning. From the outset, the authors state that their book is about design. "It is about conceiving, birthing, and conceptualizing. It is about experience and emotional attachment, utility, and appreciation."[5] They further urge their readers to abandon and lay aside their preconceived notions and models of the church

---

4. Brown and Katz, "Change by Design," 383.
5. Bergquist and Karr, *Church Turned Inside Out*, 1.

they care about and think from the inside out. Church leaders must now pay attention to specific concepts and ideas they perhaps have overlooked in the past, which should now be revisited through a whole new design of thought experiments.[6]

To tackle uDAIs' lingering immigration challenges, I will conscientiously opt for a new program designed to care for uDAIs' needs. Although the cost implication is enormous, and a variety of cases could lead to unprepared complexities that could be overwhelmingly challenging, this would be the noblest approach to help uphold the human dignity of every uDAI. My goal will be to sensitize African communities in New England to acquaint them with our numerous social and spiritual services. The aim is to use such a program to help African immigrants maximize their full human potential.

In the diocese where I belong, we do not yet have a formidable workable framework for helping African immigrants in the U.S., despite over 80 percent of our congregation members being first-generation African immigrants. My diocese is primarily handicapped because of a lack of financial resources. They are not as financially buoyant as the Episcopal Church, for instance. However, they have succeeded in providing occasional help for status modification for some clergy. These are clergy who are required to carry out the mission of church planting in the U.S. They have also provided a pocket of support for some lay members of the diocese. However, helping clergypersons is perhaps the most outstanding help offered to those seeking legal status in the U.S. that I know about in my diocese. The diocese has not yet fully developed an immigration ministry that caters for all immigrants who might be needing such help within the diocese. In that way, using one of the church renewal approaches that Bergquist and Karr suggest, I may opt for the re-alignment approach. The re-alignment approach, by definition, is an approach by which one aligns the function of an organization to its core mission. As a matter of urgency, I will re-organize the directorate in charge of immigration within the diocese so that our mission may transcend the rhetoric of personal

6. Bergquist and Karr, *Church Turned Inside Out*, 1–2.

salvation of souls and move more deeply into the transformation of whole human persons. My congregation will do this by focusing intentionally on people's genuine needs, which are physical and psychological. Doing this will portray the diocese as not just being interested in the monetary benefit that often comes from immigrant tithes, offerings, and donations but as an institution genuinely interested in the people.

I may also choose to adopt the refinement approach that does not believe in undermining existing benefits. The refinement approach, by definition, is an approach where one takes what is currently being done and makes it better. The assumption is that the diocese was already doing some great things, such as providing lectures on immigration and establishing the Cornerstone and the Good Samaritan Directorate, now called the Directorate of Care. This ministry was intended to reach out to those who are hungry, homeless, sick, in prison, etc. But as we speak, the directorate initiative is yet to fulfill its intended purpose; it is still a dormant ministry on paper. We have yet to experience this ministry's actual practicality throughout the diocese. Therefore, by utilizing the refinement approach, I will investigate the directorate's efforts by giving immigration lectures to synod delegate members—a handful of decision-makers of the diocese—and make the immigrants' ministry a diocese-wide comprehensive event with genuine compassion and a human face. The Directorate of Care will be accorded full power and rights to become an intentional ministry serving the uDAIs' needs in our diocese.

The re-alignment and the refinement approach seem much more implementable in my context because they require fewer resources than the re-designing approach, which would demand enormous costs. I will work with the finance already provided in the diocesan budget to undertake the re-alignment approach. However, my concern will be the institutional bottlenecks that will likely stifle those approaches from really taking off the ground. Although it seems very expensive and requires much hard work, the re-designing process excites me the most among the other church renewal approaches. To some extent, the sense of autonomy that my local church parish has achieved gives me this confidence because it will allow us to implement some of the ideas with reasonable liberty.

As much as I have a passion for immigrants and the challenges with which they are confronted, I still have some discouraging concerns, especially with some problematic proposals that have developed in a bid for me to help them. These requests often generate some weaknesses and almost lead me to abandon the ministry for undocumented immigrants altogether. One of the failings I observed in my own experience from the few immigration cases that I have encountered is the assumption and general tendency to think that immigrants who have become undocumented and illegal aliens are the real architects of their present predicament. We quickly forgot that these were people who left their home country mainly because of economic hardship and political instability that was not of their own making and they were forced to seek a more appropriate living environment elsewhere. These innocent immigrants are not evil in themselves but were motivated primarily by economic survival. One of the immigrants with whom I held an informal conversation was from Uganda, whom I will name Jesse (real name redacted), cited insecurity, lack of good-paying jobs, and police brutality as some of his main reasons for emigrating to the U.S. Another immigrant, from Nigeria, whom I will call Salome (real name redacted), shared the domestic violence by her husband and the need to escape continued daily brutality by him as her reason for migrating to the U.S.

Thinking a little more retrospectively, I conclude that these immigrants are not any less fortunate than our Lord Jesus. Jesus himself embodied this kind of human experience when he and his parents fled for their lives because of King Herod's tyrannical rule in their native country.[7]

---

7. Matt 2:13–14.

Immigrants' Challenges in the U.S. Today

One example of injustices against immigrants is how the church continues to react to undocumented immigrants in the U.S. Shortly after Donald Trump was sworn into office, immigration intolerance rose to a higher level. It escalated with the signing of an executive order on January 27, 2017, that threw the country and the entire world into chaos. By the contents of the executive order, restrictions were placed on seven Muslim countries. All refugee admissions were suspended for 120 days, and Syrian refugees were barred from the U.S. indefinitely.[8]

Marta Chavez argues that before 1921 there were no restrictions placed on those who emigrated to the U.S. She argues that the recent lack of tolerance towards refugees and undocumented workers is a new trend premised on the massive impact the immigrant influx is having on the country's resources and other government constituent levels.[9] The non-restriction of immigrants that Chavez refers to was the one granted to Latin Americans because they were always allowed into the U.S. before 1921, unlike Asians, who were strictly barred from having free access into the country. But Chavez is not entirely correct as California, for instance, enacted the Alien Land Law on May 3, 1913, which barred Asian immigrants from owning a piece of land. The racial bias against Asian immigrants was also amplified at the national level with the presidential support of Woodrow Wilson.[10] In May 1912 President Woodrow Wilson wrote:

> In the matter of Chinese and Japanese coolie immigration I stand for the national policy of exclusion (or

---

8. "Welcoming the Stranger," http://www.ncpolicywatch.com/2017/02/13/welcoming-stranger-christian-activist-responds-trumps-immigration-.

9. Chavez, "Latin American Migration," 8.

10. "On May 03, 1913," Equal Justice Initiative, http://calender.eji.org/racial-injustice/may/3. "The Equal Justice Initiative is a non-profit organization, based in Montgomery, Alabama, that provides legal representation to prisoners who may have been wrongly convicted of crimes, poor prisoners without effective representation, and others who may have been denied a fair trial." *Wikipedia*, https://en.wikipedia.org/wiki/Equal_Justice_Initiative.

restricted immigration) . . . We cannot make a homogeneous population out of people who do not blend with the Caucasian race . . . Oriental coolieism will give us another race problem to solve, and surely we have had our lesson.[11]

No one knows the exact figure of undocumented workers who currently reside and work in the U.S.; neither does anyone understand the influx rate. It is estimated that there are over thirteen million undocumented people, more than at any other time in modern history. There are many homeless, helpless, impoverished, and disenfranchised people craving shelter and a place where they can conduct their life's activities peacefully again.[12] However, federal immigration laws restrict the number of people migrating into the country, with the possible deportation of those found to be illegal aliens, ultimately provoking a debate between the pro-immigrant and the anti-immigrant groups. The issue suddenly becomes a contest between the rule of law and the command to stand with those discriminated against. This new contest has rekindled the "sanctuary movement" that was once prevalent in the 1980s. Rev. Alison Harrington, speaking of her concern, declared that "my scripture don't [*sic*] ask me but command me to stand with those who are being persecuted and those who are being oppressed."[13]

At the other end, the proponents of the plan to reduce the number of immigrants to the U.S., both legal and illegal, contend that the sanctuary churches are undermining the rule of law—the cornerstone of a just society.[14] But Rev. Alison Harrington, realizing that she was on the side of justice, summarized the general sentiment of the new movement by saying, ". . . again churches

11. Quoted in "On May 03, 1913," Equal Justice Initiative, http://calender. eji.org/racial-injustice/may/3.

12. Chavez, "Latin American Migration," 8–9.

13. "Sanctuary Movement," https://www.pbs.org/wnet/religionandethics/ 2017/02/03/sanctuary-movement/34422/.

14. "Sanctuary Movement," https://www.pbs.org/wnet/religionandethics/ 2017/02/03/sanctuary-movement/34422/.

and congregations across the United States are standing up to say, this is not reflective of who we believe we are as a people and this is not reflective of our faith as Christians."[15] This book is not focused on the sanctuary movement. Still, the idea of the sanctuary movement is similar and explores how the churches in the U.S. are reacting to undocumented immigrants' immigration challenges. I am yet to see African congregations, at least in New England, take a responsible role in this matter.

A Haven of Religious Liberty

Frank Lambert observed that in 1639 a group of New England Puritans drafted a constitution that accommodated their belief in God and their plan to constitute themselves as a Christian nation like their counterpart in Massachusetts Bay. The Connecticut Puritans resolved to start a "Christian Common-wealth," a proto-type nation that would depict a "city upon a hill," which could serve as an inspiration to other believers as a unique model of a nation founded on Christian principles.[16] Those Puritan fathers epitomized two distinct colonial American features: a haven for religious liberty and a nation founded on Christian precepts.

Subsequently, in 1787, the Founding Fathers of the United States of America initiated and facilitated the process of lasting legacies that clearly defined the place and the function of religion in American society. Their legacies included the notions of separation of church and state and free exercise of religion extended to people of all faiths or no faith.[17] I presupposed that this was the contextual background upon which people like Rev. Alison Harrington are anchoring their hopes and beliefs, warranting the opening of their sanctuaries to undocumented immigrants from the region of Central America. But Puritan settlers themselves

---

15. Burnett, "U.S. Churches Offer Safe Haven," https://www.npr.org/2016/02/09/466145280/u-s-churches-offer-safe-haven-for-a-new-generation-of-migrants.

16. Lambert, *Founding Fathers*, 1.

17. Lambert, *Founding Fathers*, 1–2.

had fled England because of persecution and refused to participate in religious beliefs and practices that they regarded as contravening the Scriptures. On the premise of this historical antecedent, it would be historically illegitimate for the U.S. to place restrictions on immigrants who have also fled from similar persecutions or other political injustices.[18]

Concerns raised by those who are anti-immigrant are clear and compelling. Chief among their problems is the flouting of the "law of the land." There are other concerns, such as how many immigrants should be allowed to come into the country. What will be the limit? What about the attendant effect of a massive inflow of immigrants on the country's economy, particularly when considering the vast impact such an influx will have on poor American citizenry? Some immigrants do not even know how to read and write in their indigenous languages. Consequently, some people have wondered about the viability of making citizens—contributing, happy citizens—out of the majority of these undocumented immigrants. The moral authority for creating a sanctuary of refuge and determining who is to be accepted has also generated a heated debate.[19]

The preeminent theological issue here centered on the role played by some parts of the colonies such as the New England colony. The New England colony was founded on a cornerstone of religious liberty. It retains some semblance of a nation founded on biblical legacies, which the Puritan fathers helped to nurture after fleeing persecution in England to come to the wild field of America as wandering sojourners. If this was the case, why would the United States, which adopted some of the basic national tenets that were founded on such Christian and biblical principles, neglect to obey Christ and attend to undocumented pilgrims and refugee plights even when the Bible commands disciples to help such strangers?

---

18. Lambert, *Founding Fathers*, 2.

19. "Sanctuary Movement," https://www.pbs.org/wnet/religionandethics/2017/02/03/sanctuary-movement/34422/.

Anti-immigration activists accuse sanctuary workers of breaking the law and condoning illegitimacy. Likewise, sanctuary workers have come out to defend their actions, stating that they are not violating the law; instead, the US. government has broken the law. Sanctuary workers argue that human law is supposed to reflect God's law and that any human law that contradicts divine law ought not to be obeyed. Gonzalez affirms that it was this position held by the early church Christians that accounted for their numerous deaths because they were nonconformists concerning Roman laws. Roman law required all Roman subjects to worship or venerate the emperor, which early Christians found contrary to God's law.[20] Gonzalez further argues that Jesus was a good Jew and held God's law in high esteem as a supreme gift to Israel. He also believes that the same good law could be used by some unscrupulous elements against its intended purposes. Ultimately, Gonzales defines the true meaning of the law: promoting doing good rather than evil and giving life instead of killing.[21]

All the points highlighted above effectively spotlight the reasons why churches must pursue justice for undocumented immigrants because of their marginalization and deplorable state. We must not fold our arms and allow the ongoing injustices against undocumented immigrants to persist. We have to rise and stand up for their just cause on the grounds of the dignity of every human being and the biblical injunction for us to care for the strangers in our land.

I have referred to a book that has been truly transformative for me in my pursuit of social justice for uDAIs—*In His Steps* by Charles Sheldon. This book has been remarkably insightful for me, relating to the popular movement of the late nineteenth-century and the early twentieth-century social gospel movement. The reading challenged me as a person because of my excessive focus on ensuring that my sermons were eloquently delivered. Excellent sermon delivery may be acceptable by itself, but, as graphically illustrated in the book, sermons must inspire listeners' actions. I

20. Gonzalez, "Sanctuary," 39–41.
21. Gonzalez, "Sanctuary," 41–42.

had to pause occasionally during the reading of the book to ask myself, "Am I walking in the fullness of the footsteps of Jesus?" Many things in the book spoke directly to my humanity regarding what I was supposed to do to alleviate humankind's suffering. But one crucial constructive theological feature of the social gospel that stood out for me was the need to address the structural and systemic problems in our society.

Structural and systemic problems hinder the work and the progress of any faith community, no matter how sound such a faith community might wish to be perceived as in matters of doctrine. Lack of insight into systemic marginalization and an inferior negative impact of structural policies on undocumented immigrants is a major challenge that many African church communities in New England currently face. Some African churches in New England are preoccupied with gaining more affluent membership to buy church properties rather than extending ministry outreach to the underprivileged members within the African community, especially undocumented immigrants. They are avoiding or, at best, scratching the surface of the issue. We need people like Rev. Henry Maxwell to speak out to the conscience of people so they ask themselves, "What would Jesus do in the context of uDAIs in New England?"

The Rise of African Immigrants in the U.S.

Africans first arrived in the New World on slave ships, but African immigration almost stopped after the abolition of slavery. In the years 1891–1900, only 350 Africans came to the U.S. In the first half of the twentieth century, the numbers began to increase: 31,000 Africans immigrated to the U.S. during 1900–1950.[22] The dramatic rise in the numbers of African immigrants is a more recent phenomenon. In 1970, 80,000 people living in America had been born in Africa. By 2000, that number had climbed to 880,000, and then

---

22. Arthur, *Invisible Sojourners*, 1–2.

in 2015 the Pew Research Center estimated that 2.1 million people living in the U.S. had been born in Africa.[23]

Africans who have settled in the U.S. during the last twenty years represent the largest number of Africans in more than two hundred years to settle in the U.S. Ethiopian immigrants and their children who live in the U.S. are now approximately 251,000, accounting for 0.5 percent of the total U.S. foreign-born population.[24] Between 1974 and 1995, the number of Ethiopian immigrants increased from 276 to 5,960, rising over 2,000 percent. The increase in the same period for Nigeria was from 670 in 1974 to 6,818 in 1995—over 900 percent.[25] On the other hand, Nigerian immigrants, who comprise the largest number of African immigrants in the U.S., total 376,000, their children included, accounting for about 0.6 percent of the overall U.S. foreign-born population.[26]

The rich cultural diversity of Africans has been well harmonized and was broadly publicized and accepted in the landscape of major cities across the U.S. The impact of African immigrants has been felt throughout the U.S. through their significant contributions to its cultural and economic enhancement.[27] In response to the question about why the number of Africans has continued to surge in the U.S., John Arthur outlines the following reasons in the preface of his book, *Invisible Sojourners: African Immigrant Diaspora in the United States*:

> Africa's colonial contacts with the West, the agitation for political self-determination, the cold-war, the economic and political dislocation following independence, the capitalist penetration into Africa, and the configurations

23. "Africa/United States: African Immigrant Population," https://www-proquest-com.ezproxy.bu.edu/docview/1869977515/B13E336013A64842PQ/10?accountid=9676.

24. Migration Policy Institute, "Ethiopian Diaspora in the United States," 1.

25. Arthur, *Invisible Sojourners*, vii.

26. Migration Policy Institute, "Nigerian Diaspora in the United States," 1.

27. Arthur, *Invisible Sojourners*, vii.

of U.S. immigration laws have all facilitated the immigration of Africans to the U.S.[28]

However, it is essential to note that although many of the African population in the U.S. are highly-educated elites in demand for their skills, the bulk of African immigrants that this book is concerned with were the undocumented Africans victimized by their immigration status.

Over the last four decades, Africans residing in the United States have most frequently come from Nigeria, Egypt, Ethiopia, Ghana, South Africa, Somalia, Eritrea, and Kenya.[29] African immigrants have four main reasons for coming to the United States: the desire to pursue higher education, the impulse to reunite with family members, the hope to benefit from the vast economic opportunities that the U.S. represents, and the need to escape from political tyranny and unrest.[30]

For various reasons, some of these African immigrants were undocumented. There are currently 173,000 undocumented immigrants living in Massachusetts by the estimation of the Migration Policy Institute. Nine percent of the total or about 16,000 of those people are African in origin.[31] In Rhode Island, where I preside over a second congregation in the Anglican Diocese of the Trinity (ADOTT), the estimate of total undocumented immigrants in the state is 26,000, of which 12 percent or about 3,000 are African.[32] Although not all of these uDAIs live in Everett or Providence, where the two congregations I pastor are located, many drive long distances to worship at my churches. They are

28. Arthur, *Invisible Sojourners*, vii.

29. Arthur, *Invisible Sojourners*, vii.

30. Arthur,*Invisible Sojourners*, 20.

31. "Profile of the Unauthorized Population—MA," https://www.migrationpolicy.org/data/unauthorized-immigrant-population/state/MA.

32. "Profile of the Unauthorized Population—RI," https://www.migration policy.org/data/unauthorized-immigrant-population/state/RI. Essentially, this project is not intended for religious proselytization. I expect people of other faiths to seek our services through word of mouth. The project will not discriminate against people based on religion, ethnicity, or nationality; nevertheless, the project is set up to help African undocumented immigrants primarily.

motivated to be with other Africans because of the similarities of their cultural backgrounds, even if they are not of the same ethnicity or from the same country. Many of them are also practicing Anglicans from their home country.[33]

In recent decades, exponential African immigrant growth has created resentment against them by those who fear the strain upon resources and local community capacities and other government services. There is much noise from certain quarters of the press and special interest groups who lament overstretched resources and healthcare use by immigrants. At stake is the battle between the rule of law and the biblical and theological imperatives to stand with those being victimized.[34] Trump's administration was ruthless in matters relating to the immigration discourse. However, many of Trump's immigration policies were overturned by the administration of Joe Biden.

Through my interaction with uDAIs, it became clear that they faced several challenges. First, there was much anxiety around shifting legal regulations. A January 2017 executive order comes to mind, where Trump placed movement restrictions on seven Muslim countries, suspending all refugee admission for 120 days. Although the order was stopped abruptly by a federal court, the Trump administration promised a revised version, which led to the "public charge" rule that was assented to by the Supreme Court shortly before the COVID-19 total lockdown in March 2020.[35] Such policy changes created uncertainty and left immigrants feeling vulnerable as their status in the U.S. became more tenuous. Second, uDAIs' lack of access to legal advisors due

---

33. The Anglican Diocese of the Trinity (ADOTT) is a diocese that is comprised of mainly the immigrants from Nigeria and other countries in Africa. The bishop is located in Indianapolis, Indiana. See http://www.adott.org This project does not include the many Anglicans in the African diaspora from the Caribbean.

34. Chavez, "Latin American Migration," 8–9.

35. "Welcoming the Stranger," http://www.ncpolicywatch.com/2017/02/13/welcoming-stranger-christian-activist-responds-trumps-immigration-order/; Dinan, "'Public Charge' Rule," https://www.washingtontimes.com/news/2020/feb/24/public-charge-rule-linking-welfare-use-to-green-ca/.

to insufficient funds to hire immigration lawyers exacerbated the situation. Third, undocumented immigrants also had limited economic resources because of their legal status. The only available jobs were "under the table" positions, which lack many benefits and are frequently exploitative with very low pay. Fourth, these positions lacked access to affordable healthcare, and fifth, it was a struggle to find cheap housing. The moral problem is not that these people were undocumented but that they lacked access to resources. My argument was that African churches have responsibilities to help them access some of these multiple supports. To shed more light on the challenges of uDAIs in the U.S., I will use the next section to deal extensively with the plights of undocumented immigrants through carefully crafted narratives about their daily experiences and encounters.[36]

The Fate of African Immigrants
as Sojourners in the U.S.

This section will feature some of my casual interactions with randomly selected African immigrants. These are people I have met in my ministry who are more or less friends of friends. The aim is to contextualize some of the challenges immigrants go through, especially when they have become undocumented or were on the verge of losing their temporary but limited legal status. I created a narrative for each of the immigrants with whom I interacted to have a full view of what immigrants encounter in the U.S.

To further illustrate the extent of uDAIs' problems, I initially set out to interact with scores of undocumented African immigrants, but many of them were scared of having a conversation about their immigration status. The fear of becoming an easy target by sharing their personal stories seemed to be a major stumbling block. However, I was able to find some who were

---

36. The narratives here represent my informal conversations with people. and I am not giving out their real names. They are people that cannot be identified. As anonymous informants, they are not subjects but illustrations or examples of what uDAIs experience on a day-to-day basis.

generous enough to have a candid but casual conversation with me about their present immigration status.

Jesse

Jesse (real name redacted) is from Uganda and came to the U.S. with a visitor's visa but now is a green card holder as a legal resident. He had been living in the U.S. for five years. Jesse narrated what prompted him to emigrate to the U.S. He revealed certain kinds of hardships prevalent back home in Africa that people faced as individuals, families, and communities. However, he spoke glowingly about the U.S. as a land of freedom and security. He stated that since everybody desired a good life, one of the primary reasons people come to the U.S. was for access to such opportunities; others sought freedom and security. He said, "I have flashed in my memory people who are brutalized in the name of enforcing the law, which the law enforcement agents claim to be doing by receiving the order from above. But the order the law enforcement agents follow are not orders enshrined in the country's constitution but orders that serve the selfish interest of the political leaders in power."

Jesse has been fortunate compared to the other immigrants I held informal conversations with during my private investigations. He has had a relatively smooth journey in comparison with others who have not had it so good. When he was asked how the journey has been since he first arrived in the U.S., his response was, "The U.S. is one of the best countries, if not the best country in the whole world! This is so because when you work, you get paid almost immediately, not like when you work back home in Africa, and you are not paid for a job you have done after a long while. In my case, the journey has been long, but I have been able to achieve my goals as quickly as possible." To this end, Jesse's goal and aspiration was to have a good-paying job, which has been achieved in a short while.

However, despite Jesse's firmly fixed goal, which he set out to achieve, it was not achieved without the usual work authorization challenge that immigrants experience. He narrated his basic fear and challenge in this way: "The biggest challenge for every immigrant is the challenge of being able to get a job. You know you cannot survive if you are not working even for a day. It took me a couple of months without working because it wasn't easy to get work authorization."

Although Jesse had become a green card holder at the time of our conversation, we could not complete all the questions I had in mind because the other subsequent questions may not have directly applied to him; I had to stop the conversation midway. However, his experience as an immigrant did not take away the common problems that immigrants face when they move into the Western world; he cited the endless waiting for work authorization, several months, as one example. In our brief conversation together, he also provided some good reasons people migrated using his own scenario as a case. I thanked him very much and informed him that a second casual conversation might be prompted for a follow-up if I deemed it necessary.

Salome

Salome (real name redacted) is from Nigeria and came to the U.S. with a visitor's visa but later became an illegal alien when her visa expired. Salome was a member of my congregation in one of the churches I pastor. The precarious situation that she was facing amplifies some of the fundamental challenges and threats that undocumented immigrants face in the U.S. Salome's story was one of the tragic undocumented immigrants' stories that I have listened to in recent years. For her, the road had been rough and patchy and drew considerable empathy from me. When I asked her to tell me some of the things she has encountered, her response was, "If I say 'rough,' it is an understatement! If I have my way, I think I should suffer in Nigeria rather than endure the hardship I am facing here. It has not been easy." When she was asked why she emigrated to the U.S., her response was:

It's a very long story. I left Nigeria because of domestic violence from my husband. He is entangled in an illicit relationship with another woman after about ten years into
our marriage, just after our union's first surviving child.
He would beat me up because of this woman and would
not come home for days, abandoning my only surviving
child and me. I prayed hard about the situation, thinking
that he would change, but the problem grew worse. So,
when I retired, I started coming and going out of the U.S.
I came in 2011 and 2012; then I was still working until I
relocated finally in 2017 after my retirement.

When she was asked if she understood what it means to be
undocumented, she replied, "Yes! It means you are not safe! You
cannot work, and there are a lot of fears around being undocumented. You cannot drive. When you go out, you'll walk in fear.
Even when somebody hurts you, you cannot complain because
you're undocumented". After she retired from government work
in Nigeria, Salome intended to come into the U.S. and hustle like
others by finding a job to do and then bring her daughter over
to join her. However, those plans and aspirations had not been
met. Her greatest challenges and fears were something she called
a "harvest of challenges." She was unable to mention those challenges for fear of her sister-in-law, whom she was living with at
the time. She said, "You know, I am in somebody's house, and
I am not free to fully express myself." She feared that she would
be deported back to Nigeria empty-handed one day, where she
would have to start struggling again. She had been surviving by
withdrawing her pension money from Nigeria and changing it to
dollars to meet her daily living expenses. However, the Nigerian
government has made foreign exchange extremely difficult for
people, which means she could not depend on it.

Salome did not have access to resources and support that
could help her navigate through the process of surviving while
she was still undocumented, except for the fact that she lived with
her brother's wife. That is the only support she has had. She remarked that "even when she is sick, she usually pays out of pocket
to get treatment." While still pondering on the kind of support she

received, she interjected, "Yes! The church I attend. They support with money, food, clothing, etc."

She was very optimistic that if she could get her papers to work like every other regular citizen, it would make a lot of difference because she believed she was still strong enough to work. She wanted the church to assist her in getting her paperwork to become independent.

Jambres

Jambres (real name redacted) was an international student from Nigeria who came to the U.S. with a student visa, which means she was temporarily legal but had limited access to life's necessities. Being a student with an F-1 visa status means you are legal within a time frame. You can work but not more than twenty hours a week while you are in school. However, during the holidays you are allowed to work for forty hours. When you have this status, you are always anxious and think that anything you do unknowingly would stop you from maintaining your status. She came into the U.S. to pursue a master's degree. She applied to one of the top seminaries in New England to pursue a Master of Divinity program. Although Jambres was not undocumented at the time of my interaction with her, if she was not assisted very quickly to get ordained, she would become undocumented if she overstayed the expiry of her student visa.

For her, the journey so far had been "full"—full in the sense that there had been good times and there had been bad times. It had been challenging and rewarding at the same time for her. When she first came, she realized that the system that operated in the school here was different from the one she was accustomed to in Nigeria. She made great efforts and strides to adjust to the way things were being done in America. Second, the English spoken here is different from the English she learned back home, as Nigeria was colonized by the British. Some of the terms that she used were not the same or did not mean the same things. And things that did not have an offensive meaning back home meant something offensive here. She said,

> For example, the word "half-cast." Back home, when you say "half-cast," it means a product of a black and white person or black and a different race. But using that term here, someone let me know that it is derogatory. Here, they use the term mixed-race or biracial. Even a term like "living room," which we sometimes call a "parlor" back home, means a bar or something here. So, I started to adjust to the terms here because you could be misunderstood if you use the wrong term in communicating. I also faced racism, which I had to fight personally with the support of other colleagues, because here the system is organized to favor a group of people over and above others, even when you demonstrate that you're more competent and possess a superior qualification above them.

Jambres had thought that when she finished her master's degree, she would get a job. But getting a job was hard because she realized that you need a authorization to work even when you are a legal immigrant. She criticized the bottlenecks around the system that sometimes make it hard for immigrants to survive. She said, "I expected things to be better here than back home, like getting things very fast and on merit. But it is not exactly like that. You can merit something but someone who you are better than can take it because they belong to a certain class or a certain group of people." Still wallowing in deep disappointment, Jambres had not found a job as she had earlier planned because she went back to school. She earned her Master of Divinity degree, an accomplishment for which she is grateful to God. She stated enthusiastically that "I am still marching forward trying to do the right things, being on the right track, and hope for the best." She recognized financial challenges as her biggest challenge. She expressed some of the limitations she has as a student. She said,

> As a student, you are only allowed to work in school. Unfortunately, those jobs are already taken by domestic students. Another is the inability to get support for loans or scholarships. The Trump factor was another fear,

especially for every immigrant. Now that Trump is out of the way, we are hoping that this new administration will be lenient to international people and help us to have a way to settle down. Would they do something that will benefit me? Would they put out policies that will enable me to start my process of gaining permanent legal residency? These are the concerns I have at this moment.

When Jambres was asked if she had access to resources and support that could help her navigate herself, particularly as she planned to transition from her current status to a permanent legal resident, her response was, "Yes and no!" She had been trying to be ordained in a church, and if she gets ordained, the church would file an application for her visa, not financially but as a recognized member of the church. However, if anything went wrong, she would be back to square one. However, she mentioned that she enjoyed some kind of support from her mentors and church members, but their support could not change her status. They could only help by giving her work to do but strictly within the legal frame.

She mentioned the type of resources and support that she thought are needed to help her. She stated, "If the government can help reinstate the former policy that helps people get their green card, so far they have not committed a crime or been sentenced for one, that will be nice. Again, it will be helpful if churches could help people like me who want to become an ordained minister by creating a smooth path for me instead of creating difficulties for such processes." She wanted the churches to meet the immigrants where they are by having, for example, a committee that looked into the plights of immigrants. The church should have known the recent things that were happening in the world of these immigrants. They should have become aware of what was going on in the life of these immigrants, like being in the frontline for them. The church should have helped immigrants who worked for them who were not pursuing ordination. She said, "Most people in the churches—I don't want to say they don't care, but I don't feel it where I am."

Emmanuella

Emmanuella (real name redacted) is a Nigerian who came to the U.S. to further her education. However, due to a lack of funds or a significant scholarship, she was unable to fulfill her dream. She dropped out of school until her F-1 status expired and subsequently became undocumented. The journey had been very tough for Emmanuella, who used to hope to enroll in medical school. She underscored the challenges she had to face to adapt and adjust to her new status as an illegal immigrant. She found it difficult to make new friends because of her status as an illegal alien. She had applied for a green card previously but was denied. She was then preoccupied with the fear of being rejected again because, according to her, she had been applying for years. Emmanuella was hopeful that she might still one day get back to medical school and ultimately be able to make an impact in the lives of others through her profession as a medical doctor. This was still essentially an unmet aspiration, but she was grateful to God that some of her plans were now being fulfilled. She mentioned the fact that she has the service of an attorney who was providing legal support for her, helping her to navigate the transition from her current undocumented status to becoming a permanent legal resident. She said in her own words, "Yes, I have a lawyer and I am on the road to getting a green card." She had implored churches to educate their potential members on what needs to be done to obtain citizenship. She wanted churches to help with the services of attorneys, and have an organization expressly set up to cater for the immigrants through fund-raising.

Joseph

Joseph (real name redacted) came into the U.S. with a visitor's visa but allowed his visa to expire because his primary purpose for coming into the U.S. was for a better life. He wanted to live out his dream of helping humanity through his endowed gifts and skills. He, however, confessed that the journey had not been as easy as he had initially thought. He was not about to be deterred and give up on his dreams. He had dreamed of positively affecting his generation, learning the dynamics of living in a pluralistic society like the U.S., and escaping the security challenges that are threatening the common person back home in Africa. Joseph's aspirations and hopes had not all been met, but he was ever cheerful and continued to push for the realization of his dreams. His current challenge now was his inability to get the right job rather than the "under the table" kind of work because of his illegal status. He also feared that he might fall into the hands of the police and the immigration patrol officers who might engineer his deportation back to Africa. Currently, Joseph was without any support or access to resources that could help him navigate the transition process of illegal status to become a permanent resident. But he could identify some of the resources that would be helpful for him, such as legal advice, immigration counseling, and confidential listeners who would be empathetic to his story. A few organizations had helped him in the past, such as the Yoruba Association in Boston, Boston Community Church. He believed that churches could further help undocumented immigrants by providing a platform for advising them; this could be legal advice and organizing confidential programs for them where the undocumented could open up to get the right direction to change their status. He said churches could also provide financial support for undocumented immigrants and engage their services as volunteer workers.

Charisa

Charisa (real name redacted) arrived in the U.S. with a visitor's visa and allowed it to expire, thus became an illegal immigrant. She had initially emigrated with the expectation of a better life, but life had been very tough for her since she became an undocumented immigrant. She had naively believed that getting a green card would be easy, but it turned out to be untrue. She had thought that once she got her green card she would become a happy and contributing citizen for the country and to her church. She was disappointed that her hopes and aspirations had not been met because she came to realize that the fulfillment of all her dreams would be dependent on her being a legally recognized immigrant. She mentioned some of the challenges and fears she had, such as lack of freedom to express herself fully like a free citizen. She also feared deportation. She even claimed that she felt incomplete, like something was missing in her life, a feeling of emptiness. She did not feel like a fulfilled person because of her illegal status. Charisa thought the service of a trusted attorney was needed to help her navigate the complex process of transition to permanent residency. She was frustrated by her inability to find organizations that could have been of help to her. However, she believed that the churches could have helped un-documented immigrants by providing the platform with the right resources and support to process their green cards.

Julius

Julius (real name redacted) arrived in the U.S. with a visitor's visa. His primary purpose for coming into the country was to make money and experience a better life in America. He wanted to live the American dream. After a few weeks, he realized that living the American dream was not an easy task. He remarked that "it is not working out as I thought." At the time of Julius sharing his experience, he still had a legal right to stay in the U.S. but risked becoming an undocumented immigrant if he continued to remain in the country after the expiry of the visa issued to him. Julius had planned to get a legal and lucrative job, get his social security num-ber, and live like a regular citizen when he first arrived. But his sudden realization was that achieving those milestones involved a longer process than he had initially thought and imagined. He feared he might not get a full-time job, which meant he might end up doing work without a work permit. He was beginning to feel the heat of facing deportation if he was found out to be an illegal alien. Julius did not have any access to resources and support to help him navigate himself through the transition from his current sta-tus of becoming a legal resident. He did not have any organization's support at the time we spoke. He hoped to be connected to helpful resources and support someday. He had identified finances and trusted attorneys as some of the types of resources that might have been helpful to him. He wanted churches to help people like him financially and by offering spiritual support.

Benedict

Benedict (real name redacted) is an undocumented immigrant who came into the U.S. for improved life prospects. He overstayed the visitor's visa he had when he first came to the U.S. Things had not been as easy as he had thought. He struggled to make ends meet. He planned to start working immediately after he arrived and make money, but things did not go as planned. He only then realized that he needed first to find a way to get his papers and become a legal resident before starting to think of work. Benedict was concerned about how long it would take to get his green card, which is not easily predictable. He was battling with the harsh reality that he might be deported from the U.S. if he was found to be an illegal alien.

Benedict claimed to have access to partial information to help him navigate his way out of the present predicament. However, he had identified money and a trustworthy attorney as the critical requirements to process the correct information on immigration issues available to him. He wanted churches to provide financial assistance and spiritual support to African immigrants who may need such help.

Judith

Judith (real name redacted) fled her home country with her mother because of political unrest. When she arrived, things were really tough for her, but she soon began to find her feet, especially when she began to participate in the Redeemed Christian Church of God parish in Boston. The church accepted her with open arms, providing shelter for her and her mother. She hoped that very soon she would be able to meet other family members and no longer be separated from them as in the past. Judith's hope was not mere optimism but a hope based on the fact that she had just received her work permit but was still without a social security number. She expected that everything would soon work out well so that she could see her other family members from whom she had been separated for a long time. She believed that for an undocumented immigrant to make progress in this country, the service of a competent legal expert is required. She wanted the churches to help undocumented immigrants with financial support, provide the platform for the service of compassionate attorneys, and offer spiritual guidance.

Joyce

Joyce (real name redacted) has been in the U.S. since 2008. Her purpose for emigrating was to seek a better life. When she first arrived, she came with a visitor's visa, which later expired and subsequently she became an undocumented immigrant. Joyce recounted her experience and exclaimed that the journey had been very rough. Thirteen years after she first arrived, she was still struggling, unable to get a job and decent housing. She was working on her change of status but lacked the proper support or sufficient access to relevant information that could have helped her. More than anything, Joyce wanted a full-time job to end all the financial troubles she had been facing since 2008. She wanted churches to create a forum where seasoned immigration attorneys could educate immigrants, especially those who had become undocumented or were on the verge of becoming undocumented.

Fisher

Fisher (real name redacted) was born in South Africa and came into the U.S. with a visitor's visa, which later expired, making him an illegal alien. His purpose for coming to the U.S. was to experience a better life for himself and his family. Since he first arrived, life had been challenging, particularly with finding suitable accommodation, getting a legal job, and driving from point A to B, which had been impossible for him because of his immigration status. Fisher's aspirations were numerous, including becoming a good citizen, finding a good job, and becoming a professional in his chosen career path. He was optimistic that those aspirations were about to be fulfilled. Fisher revealed other challenges he was currently facing, such as lack of access to the correct information that could have helped him navigate his present status to a permanent legal resident quickly. He shared having to confront intimidation from people because of his status as an undocumented immigrant. He was constantly being haunted by wondering where his next meal would come from. Fisher did not have any form of support. Neither did he know the type of support he needed to begin his transition process to become a permanent legal resident. He, however, believed that churches could help undocumented immigrants with accommodation, feeding, and spiritual guidance and support.

Linda

Linda (real name redacted) was born in Liberia but later moved to the U.S. to experience a better life and further her education. She first came to the U.S. with a visitor's visa, which later expired, which meant that she became an undocumented immigrant. The journey had been relatively good, according to her. She had hoped to become a medical doctor someday. Her challenge was her status as an illegal alien, which was preventing her admission to medical school. She feared being deported if her status remained unchanged in the near future. She claimed she did not have access to resources and support to help her navigate the transition process and did not know how to go about it. She, however, said that the church she was attending in Providence, Rhode Island, had been very helpful to her in a small way. She believed that churches could help undocumented immigrants with attorney fees to secure legal documents, even if it was going to be in the form of a loan.

Hazael

Hazael (real name redacted) came into the U.S. in 2001 on a visitor's visa, which had since expired. He had been an undocumented immigrant for twenty years, a status that had negated his desire to seek a better life. Although he claimed that things had not been too bad for him since he first arrived, he had been stuck in one place, unable to advance his life because he could not get legal papers and a work permit like other regular citizens. He was still optimistic that things would become okay for him one day, but none of his hopes and aspirations had been fulfilled. Hazael is a religious person and has a firm belief in God to settle him at his own appointed time. The only identified need for Hazael was to get a work permit so he could start working and paying his bills like other citizens. He was grateful for the help and support he had enjoyed in his church spiritually, physically, and financially. He thought that the church's help was minimal unless the U.S. government stood up to their responsibility by making life comfortable for everyone irrespective of their countries of origin.

Jacintha

Jacintha (real name redacted) came to the U.S. for a better life and to work so that she could provide support for her family back home. She came on a visitor's visa that later expired, rendering her an undocumented immigrant. The journey has been full of ups and downs and sometimes very frustrating, particularly since she realized how important it was to get a work permit to do legal work. She recounted numerous occasions she had been taken advantage of by people because she did not have legal documents to work and remain in the country. Other challenges were accommodation and payment of utilities. She seriously dreaded being deported due to her continued illegal presence in the U.S. She, however, wanted the

U.S. government to grant amnesty to undocumented immigrants across the country, especially those of them working very hard to find a job and make ends meet. She hoped that the Biden administration would fulfill their pledge to grant the over thirteen million undocumented immigrants in the U.S. an easy path to citizenship. Jacintha wanted the churches to stand up for them and be strong advocates for undocumented immigrants in matters relating to their dignity as human beings and permanent residency.

The Way Forward

It was evident from all the stories above that uDAIs were facing hard times in the U.S. Some of them were not even treated as full human beings due to their immigration status. The oppression and the marginalization they faced from other people more fortunate than they were sometimes became unimaginable. But these undocumented immigrants were created in God's image just like every other regular citizen and their precarious situations were once embodied by Jesus Christ himself—God in the flesh. Therefore, we should have a renewed perspective about the plights of undocumented immigrants and remember that whatever we do for the least of these brethren, we have done it to Jesus himself.

African churches in the U.S. should rise and stop their egomaniacal style of ministry and get into the neighborhood and seek out genuine immigrants with real needs and take the ministry to them. African churches needed to act like the good shepherd who went out to seek and laid his life down for the sheep. The stories of these undocumented immigrants should drive us to ask what Jesus would do for these people if he was in our position.

Based on my conversations with uDAIs and from their narratives above, I have come to realize that these people are not necessarily asking for too much from churches. They only want the churches to become aware that they need information that will help them navigate and survive a bureaucratic society like the U.S. They need assistance with legal advice, financial support whenever it is possible for churches to make that available, and of course, spiritual support and companionship as much as possible.

Chapter 2

Cultural Shifts and the Influence of the Social Gospel Movement

Introduction

MY UNDERSTANDING OF THE traditional church setting has been challenged in recent years, not because it is inherently evil but because of a shift in my worldview. I do not believe that the church should be organized and practiced the way I did initially, twenty years ago, when I still had a closed worldview about personal salvation as the only way of transforming people. In recent years, I have seen the shortcomings of emphasizing individual salvation to the detriment of social salvation, which is more systemic and structural in approach.

I grew up in a traditional faith community setting with strong emphases on intense weekly Bible study, weekly prayer meetings, daily house-to-house evangelism, and weekly church workers' meetings. These activities aimed to ensure that I was spiritually in tune with God and promoted the interest of the gospel of Christ. Unfortunately, I had no time to think about what to make of my life as a member of the global community. The results of being involved in a church community with many formal structured activities were not what they intended, in my case, but rather the unintended products of being part of a living fellowship.

I enjoyed those activities for most of my Christian life and still do when the opportunities present themselves to me to practice them. However, in the last five years of my theological graduate study, I have had those firmly held theological beliefs challenged, but not because I doubted my faith in the gospel of Christ. The problem for me is the tension between the faith community as I had previously known it and the challenges of building a contemporary faith community today with emerging contexts.

Church without Walls

One concept that has been fascinating to me in the last five years is the concept of the *church without walls*.[1] The idea does not emphasize those who come to the church building itself, but those who do not, require going to the church building itself for transformation in their lives (John 4:19–24). Pondering on Anderson, Petersen, and Shelley's "Church without Walls," what does it mean to function within a church structure without imposing the traditional meaning and creating walls? I concluded that a church without walls is a plausible idea to accommodate in my ministry. Perhaps the "four walls model" was a creation of necessity and not necessarily the New Testament's intention, as Frank Viola argued throughout his book *Reimaging Church: Pursuing the Dream of Organic Christianity*. Viola writes:

> A revolution in both the theology and practice of the church is upon us. Countless Christians, including theologians, ministers, and scholars, are seeking new ways to

1. The idea of church without walls was initially borrowed from the Bible in Zechariah 2:4, where it says that "Jerusalem will be a city without walls because of the great number of people . . ." It was then applied to the variety of activities that a church could do that will extend beyond personal salvation of people to social salvation through some form of social activism. Steve Rabey in his article "Church without Walls" mentioned three authors who were pioneering thinkers of this concept: Leith Anderson, Jim Petersen, and Bruce Shelley. Rabey, "Church without Walls."

renew and reform the church. Others have given up on the traditional concept of church altogether. They have come to the conviction that the institutional church as we know it today is not only ineffective, but it's also without biblical merit. For this reason, they feel it would be a mistake to reform or renew the present church structure. Because the structure is the root problem.[2]

Viola presents a new paradigm for the church, founded on the New Testament concept that the church of Jesus is a spiritual organism, not an institutional organization.[3] Similarly, Steve Rabey likened the church without walls concept to a traveler trying to book a flight to the Soviet Union, but bent on using an outdated map. A travel agent told him that the Soviet Union belongs to the past, having been replaced by fifteen sovereign countries. Unfortunately, the would-be traveler will hear none of it, saying, "This can't be. It's right here on my map!" Rabey argues that many leaders try to chart a path for the church of Jesus Christ by using outmoded analyses and traditions.[4]

Cultural Shifts and the New Contexts for the Church

About seven years ago, a parishioner of a church I was attached to in Cambridge, Massachusetts, offered me a free ride to my home immediately after the church service. As soon as we proceeded on the journey, we began to have a conversation about some of the changes that were taking place in our modern society. Specifically, we had discussions about the younger generation's worldviews and their ability to get instant information on their smartphone, just with a few clicks, something not so readily available to previous generations. We recognized that these capabilities are transforming and influencing how millennials are making decisions. But their parents and grandparents could not make such

2. Viola, *Reimaging Church*, 15.

3. Viola, *Reimaging Church*, 16.

4. Rabey, "Church without Walls."

instantaneous decisions when they were younger because such electronic devices did not yet exist.

Some religious leaders have complained about people's commitment to traditional church paraphernalia that involves Bible study, prayer meetings, house-to-house evangelism, church workers' meetings, etc. They see the failure of people committing to these activities as a sign of rebellion against God. But I have a different view; what we are witnessing is only a shift in how people want to be organized and reached on spiritual matters.

Millennials and GenZ have too much information at their fingertips, causing them to make some informed but also uninformed choices about God and the things of the kingdom. Because times have changed, I am persuaded that today's community of faith and the future communities would not necessarily embrace the ideas of the more traditional faith community in which I grew up. The rate of change, for instance, in the last twenty-five years, has been more dramatic and rapid than the changes we witnessed over the previous hundred years before the beginning of the twenty-first century.[5] The changes are evolving new contexts that are no longer agreeable with earlier contexts that existed when I was growing up, which also hold for the generations before mine. Current contexts have forced me to rethink how Jesus would live out ministry if he were present in this day and age. For instance, from my biblical understanding, Jesus was a new kind of rabbi, defying the traditional rabbi's norms. He spoke about real-life issues and daily encounters of people in the marketplace, on the high mountainside, in the plain, in the synagogues and the temple. Every occasion provided Jesus with a context to perform ministry. He performed ministry activities within the four walls of the synagogue and more of such activities in the neighborhood context. The neighborhood is where people with real needs are ever present.

5. The change referred to here is the advent of the internet worldwide connectivity that has made instant communication possible to any person anywhere in the world, which has also made the global economy accessible to every global citizen without the trans-border barriers that existed for most of the twentieth century.

Similarly, I wonder if Jesus were present at this moment, how he would handle social media. What would information technology mean to Jesus? Would he embrace it or detest it? The tension really for me is would ministry be limited to the church's walls? Or is something else happening that will recognize ministry taking place within the neighborhood outside the "four walls model"?

These emerging new ministry contexts impel me to pursue a neighborhood transformation among uDAIs. Furthermore, I intend to do this with the theological framework of Rauschenbusch's new kind of evangelism. Rauschenbusch was a classic social gospel adherent, who favored the new form of evangelism to the old form of evangelism.[6]

The Social Gospel in Practice

The mark of a true church for me is getting into the neighborhood and transforming it as Jesus did for most of his earthly ministry. The notion of neighborhood transformation is derived from reading Revelation 21, where verses 3–4 emphasize that God is moving into the neighborhood and making his home with men and women! Of course, the intention is to wipe away every tear from their eyes and relieve them of pain. In the same spirit, I want this type of neighborhood transformation to be accomplished in my ministry by fulfilling the injunction of Christ to feed the hungry, shelter the homeless, clothe the naked, visit the sick, and help strangers.[7]

Carrying out this assignment is not only going out to look for hungry people, sick people, or naked people. A more strategic approach could entail tackling these problems structurally and targeting the oppressive systems that create social injustice. Harry Emerson Fosdick said that "any church that pretends to care for the souls of people but is not interested in the slums that damn them . . . promotes a dry, passive, do nothing religion in need of new blood."[8]

---

6. Rauschenbusch, "New Evangelism," 137.

7. Matt 25:35–40 (KJV).

8. Fosdick, *Hope of the World*, 25.

For this reason, the social gospel movement has been my motivation while also inspiring me to pursue a worthy ministry that caters for the immigration needs of uDAIs in New England.

In 1958, Martin Luther King Jr. echoed a similar sentiment by crediting his understanding of the civil rights movement to the social gospel movement of the late nineteenth century and early twentieth century in American religious history. He acknowledged the influence of early-twentieth-century church leaders like Walter Rauschenbusch, whose social gospel had pushed Christian theology beyond the concern for individual salvation to engage questions of social justice.[9] The social gospel as a movement is primarily associated with late-nineteenth and early-twentieth-century American Protestantism. Other leading American pastors and theologians were active in the social gospel movement during 1890–1945: Shailer Matthews, Washington Gladden, Richard Ely, and Charles Sheldon.

Numerous scholars have linked the origin of the classic social gospel tradition to the progressive period of the late nineteenth and early twentieth centuries. Besides, many of these religious scholars since that time have made efforts to exchange views on what should be the exact definition of the term "social gospel." There have been many definitions given by different scholars who attempted to capture the essential parts of what the social gospel should entail, but the one that seems to be widely accepted was the one offered by Shailer Matthews: "the application of the teaching of Jesus and the total message of the Christian salvation to society, the economic life, and social institutions such as the state, family, as well as to individuals."[10]

The social gospel movement was a spin-off of the theological liberalism that embraced a progressive theological ideology and fits it into the American socio-political and economic landscape. The tradition is strongly connected with the emergence of the Protestant theological adherents of the late nineteenth and early twentieth centuries. It combines both the evangelical and liberal

9. Evans, *Social Gospel in American Religion*, 1.

10. Smith, *Dictionary of Religion and Ethics*, 416–17.

theological heritage to promote American institutions' systemic and structural changes. Since its inception, the movement was widely known to have impacted the religious landscape and society at large, cumulatively reaching its apex during the civil rights movement in the 1950s and 1960s.[11] Without a doubt, the classic social gospel tradition has many strengths that are worthy of attention. The two most essential arguments advanced by the movement, which I will discuss further in this book, are its arguments on structural and systemic reform and applying the golden rule to every human's endeavors.

First, the argument for structural and systemic change, which was well presented in fictional form in Charles Sheldon's books *In His Steps* and *The Crucifixion of Philip Strong*, was one crucial feature of the social gospel that stood out for me. The arguments from both books directly addressed the structural and systemic problems causing rottenness and decay within society. *In His Steps* demonstrated many Christians' deceptive behaviors toward societal ills and moral bankruptcy while they attempted to justify their actions by their lackadaisical attitude. He argued that a good number of Christians always engage in the act of passing the buck by saying, "It's not my fault," without anyone stopping the buck-passing at his/her table. This was the nauseating attitude depicted in Rev. Henry Maxwell's fictional story and his affluent congregation of the First Church of Raymond.[12] Later their deceit and vainglory were exposed by a shabby-looking young man who was not even expected to be part of their service but came to the day's service uninvited. The man had been jobless for ten months, and his effort to get another job met with a series of disappointments and a lack of responsiveness from the so-called Christian people.[13] His wife died along the way, and his only daughter had to live with another family while he tried to find another job. Above all, after his highly thought-provoking and convicting speech, the

11. Evans, *Social Gospel*, 2–3.

12. Sheldon, *In His Steps* 14–16.

13. Sheldon, *In His Steps*, 8–16.

man fell and died in the First Church of Raymond.[14] It was not until then that Rev. Henry Maxwell understood that his ministry had not been very much concerned about the marginalized and the oppressed people of his community. He quickly rallied around his members and challenged them, saying, "I want volunteers from the First Church who will pledge themselves, earnestly and honestly for an entire year not doing anything without first asking the question, "what would Jesus do?" And after asking that question, each one will follow Jesus as strictly as he knows how, no matter what the result may be."[15] The result was a massive shift in how many of his church's affluent members dealt with some of the endemic social ills with which they had long been confronted within their community.

Likewise, in Charles Sheldon's second book, *The Crucifixion of Philip Strong,* I read how Philip Strong, another fictional character, rejected the invitation to go to Elmdale, where he could easily indulge himself with an empty display of intellectual sagacity. Instead, he opted to receive the call to serve the church in Milton, where there was the opportunity to solve a real problem like the labor question facing the people in that neighborhood. He seemed to have a strong urge to act as a prophetic voice speaking to the down-trodden and changing the society, and Milton Church looked a perfect fit for such a change. Philip Strong soon began to exhibit glimpses of this after his resumption at Milton. He announced to his congregation that he would be starting a series of monthly talks on "Christ and Modern Society." He planned to speak as Christ would speak about modern society—its sins and everyday concerns.[16]

Apart from Charles Sheldon's fictional writings, another strong voice who propagated the notion of structural and systemic change was Rauschenbusch. He had a radical view of "new evangelism" as opposed to the old evangelism, which professed an

---

14. Sheldon, *In His Steps,* 16–17.

15. Sheldon, *In His Steps,* 23–24.

16. Sheldon, "Crucifixion of Philip Strong," 6.

individual's repentance from sin but neglects the people's social degradation.[17] He argued that:

> The powerlessness of the old evangelism is only the most striking and painful demonstration of the general state of the churches. Its causes are not local nor temporary. It does not lie in a lack of hard work, prayer, or keen anxiety. It lies in the fact that modern life has gone through immense changes and the church has not kept pace with it in developing the latent moral and spiritual resources of the gospel, which are needed by the new life.[18]

Rauschenbusch was optimistic that the new evangelism, if permitted to flourish, would overcome these hurdles and unleash the gospel's full weight, which would no longer be the responsibility of a single man but a collective endeavor of many sincere men.[19] He reiterated further that the new evangelism would have to retain all that was true and good in the old evangelism and move the human understanding of salvation closer to the divine origin. He foresaw a new vision of God, of life, of duty, of destiny, to which the best religious life of our era would surrender. The new evangelism could help us conceive how a Christian man should order his life under this new atmosphere and demand the same from others.[20]

Rauschenbusch contrasted his generation's civilization with that of the Graeco-Roman Empire, whose rapid decline was preceded by a golden era. He saw the rise of stupendous wealth in the twentieth century as a defining mark that resembled the rise of the Graeco-Roman Empire. He argued that the second century of his era seemed to be the culmination of the past glory era of the Graeco-Roman Empire in countless ways (the assertion of Rauschenbusch still holds even in the twenty-first century, which has witnessed more wealth and technological sophistication). The empire seemed indestructible and would likely endure for another thousand years of power and glory, he imagined. To envision the

17. Rauschenbusch, "New Evangelism,"137.
18. Rauschenbusch, "New Evangelism," 142.
19. Rauschenbusch, "New Evangelism," 143.
20. Rauschenbusch, "New Evangelism," 137.

fall would be like predicting the apocalyptic end of humanity and our civilization.[21] Stated differently, Rauschenbusch argued that nations do not usually slow down in progress because of prosperity but by the continued systemic promotion of injustice. He posited that education, art, wealth, and culture might gain real momentum and even attain a state of perfection. But then the cankerworm of social injustice may already have wreaked havoc at the nation's moral fabric until the decadence is ultimately exposed either by internal implosions or external catastrophes.[22] This is a wake-up call to American Christians and the U.S. government that they cannot continue to promote injustice and systemic marginalization of undocumented immigrants. It is for this reason that I have a desire to pursue a new form of evangelism to cater for their needs as proposed by Rauschenbusch.

In *Christianizing the Social Order*, Rauschenbusch's primary concern was if there would still be Christian people advocating for the plight of the poor, widows, and the marginalized. He was skeptical that it would be a kind of "faith" that would be lost in private devotion to God while neglecting the concern for the neighbor. The handwriting on the wall of many Christian people is their total loss in private devotion to God and church activities. But he genuinely advocated that we live out our true Christian calling when we engage in social and just societal causes.[23]

Rauschenbusch's optimism did not make him live in the self-disillusionment of a perfect and utterly just society. He knew that there was no perfection for humans in this life but a possible growth toward perfection. He professed that a perfect social life may be somewhat elusive but can still be sought out in faith. Human suffering may not be eradicated, but through hard work can be made to be non-existence because "God's kingdom is always but coming."[24]

---

21. Rauschenbusch, "New Evangelism," 145–47.

22. Rauschenbusch, "New Evangelism," 148.

23. Rauschenbusch, "Christianizing the Social Order," 169.

24. Rauschenbusch, "New Evangelism," 65.

The Golden Rule—"Do unto Others as
You Want Them to Do unto You"

The second important argument of the classic social gospel is Richard T. Ely and Washington Gladden's golden rule. In Gladden's imagination, he dreamed of a perfect human in an ideal society. He envisioned an ideal society of Christians demonstrating the law of love as a regulating principle for their socio-economic and political framework as well as in the industrial workplace. Evans argued that Gladden and Ely's central thesis was that every human would genuinely display the spirit of benevolence toward one another if the golden rule were upheld.[25] However, Gladden traced the relationship between labor and capital back in history to establish the golden rule's potency. The idea was to differentiate the effective systems through which labor and capital have interacted throughout history. He was preoccupied with finding a systematic way of resolving the strife between labor and capital. Gladden by this approach demonstrated that he cared for the capital provider as much as he cared for the labor. However, some critics would not agree with him because of his affiliation to a labor union.[26]

Richard T. Ely reflected on the golden rule by using Matthew 25:31–46 as his primary text and context. He posed a question and attempted to answer it as best as he could; he asked, "what is the most noteworthy feature in the narrative: namely, the exquisite beauty of the humanitarianism which it breathes. It is the gospel of humanity because it is the gospel of the Son of man."[27] He argued that the implementation and non-implementation of social duties in the Gospel narrative separated the blessed from the cursed. Ely recognized this theological understanding as something very radical and new within the religious system. He saw it as sarcasm when religiously opinionated people elevated the love of God far above the love of their neighbor, especially when they did not see doing

25. Evans, *Social Gospel*, 21.

26. Gladden, "Labor and Capital."

27. Ely, *Social Aspects of Christianity*, 4–5.

God's services through human sacrifices.[28]Ely asserted that "nothing is more difficult, nothing more requires divine grace than the constant manifestation of love to our fellows in all our daily acts, in our buying, selling, getting gain."[29]

Weaknesses of the Social Gospel Movement

As important as the social gospel adherents described in this book are, regrettably, they also demonstrated some notable weaknesses. These social gospel adherents were weak in their lack of emphasis on racial injustices and discrimination. The movement itself resulted in declines in church membership and a lack of spiritual hunger for evangelism.

One area where criticism emerged from predominantly white Protestant churches was the gross insensitivity to racial injustice and discrimination. No one mentioned racism and the pervasive nature of white privileges during their days. The writings of some of the social gospel adherents were instrumental to the African American movements as they advanced toward racial justice. But those writings were slightly modified to suit their intended purpose in the fight against racism. However, these social gospel scholars themselves did not deem it fit to give racism critical attention and a respectable space in their discourse.[30]

Another weakness of the classic social gospel was its tendency to degenerate quickly into loss of church membership because of excessive focus on social advocacy. It lacked mass appeal to a lot of people. Mass appeal is very crucial to popular evangelicalism. The classic social gospel erroneously seemed to see social advocacy as the church's primary calling.[31]

The main result of this chapter is that I have experienced a shift in my worldview, which is a response to how modern and

---

28. Ely, *Social Aspects of Christianity*, 5.
29. Ely, *Social Aspects of Christianity*, 6.
30. Evans, *Social Gospel*, 11.
31. Evans, *Social Gospel*, 13.

future faith communities want to be organized because of the changing ministry contexts. This has developed a desire in me after being inspired by certain classic social gospel adherents to pursue a new kind of evangelism among uDAIs that focuses on their social improvement. I am very aware that social gospel movement had some inherent weaknesses, which were already highlighted. Still, it remains one of the most valuable theological education tools that has become a ministry asset to me in all my years of graduate training.

Chapter 3

The Theological and Biblical Vision for Neighborhood Transformation

Introduction

THIS CHAPTER WILL DESCRIBE my theological and biblical vision for neighborhood transformation. The premise upon which I will be executing neighborhood transformation is the biblical transformation vision of the prophet Isaiah in Isaiah 61, and another important biblical passage, Revelation 21. These two biblical references sum up my mission and calling to initiate a neighborhood transformation that fulfills the injunction of Christ to feed the hungry, shelter the homeless, clothe the naked, visit the sick, and help strangers according to Matthew 25:35–40.

The chapter will also focus on the notion of incarnation, which is one of the most significant revelations of the Bible that also shapes how I intend to take the vision of neighborhood transformation to African immigrants in New England. It is a fantastic idea and it is about the idea of God being with us, which the prophet Isaiah called "Immanuel," interpreted as "God with us."[1]

---

1. Isa 7:14; Matt 1:23 (KJV).

I am going to rely on my own experience and how other people like Mark R. Gornik and Maria Liu Wong, the authors of the book *Stay in the City: How Christian Faith Is Flourishing in an Urban World*, as well as Samuel Wells and Howard Thurman understood neighborhood transformation. I specifically choose these theologians as my main conversation partners because of our common theological heritage and tradition as well as the inspiration I have drawn from their work. The work of Mark R. Gornik and Maria Liu Wong is focused on being present with our neighbors, while the work of Samuel Wells is focused on being with our marginalized neighbors. Similarly, Howard Thurman helps me to think about fulfilling the mission of God among the underprivileged in the neighborhood.

I will begin this chapter by exploring the nature of neighborhood transformation. Then I will try and conclude with what I consider to be my vision of the connectivity between the New Jerusalem and the African immigrant "neighborhood."

What Is Neighborhood Transformation?

Neighborhood transformation has been one of my passions since 1998, and it has been my principal passion for the last seven years. A burning desire to feed the hungry, clothe the naked, shelter the homeless, visit the sick, and help strangers[2] has guided my ministry since 1998, but recently with more intentionality. According to the availability of funds, the two churches that I pastor were already involved in these biblical deeds to some extent. Our church family has been very deliberate in our attempt to reach out to African immigrants, especially the undocumented, to provide a safe place for them. My ministry intentionally seeks out those that could be regarded as strangers. My ultimate goal is to turn such people from the emerging African immigrant community in the New England neighborhood into our neighbors—this is my conceptual understanding of the usage of the term "neighborhood transformation."

2. Matt 25:35–40 (KJV).

We are now on the path of starting a distinct non-profit organization that will be charged solely with the responsibility of providing resources and support for these African immigrant strangers.

My church program is taken in tandem with the prophet Isaiah's vision for the Israelites in exile to transform their neighborhood. The scriptural passage quoted below is one passage that has been a driving force for me for more than twenty years. It encourages me to be involved in changing my neighborhood, transforming it and making it more habitable for our African immigrant brothers and sisters who have fled political tyranny back in Africa to seek a better life. Together we shall rebuild the old ruins, raise a new city out of the wreckage (a new African immigrant community that is free from oppression and subjugation). Here is the experience of the prophet Isaiah for the people of Israel in exile.

> The Spirit of God, the Master, is on me because God anointed me. He sent me to preach good news to the poor, heal the heartbroken, announce freedom to all captives, pardon all prisoners. God sent me to announce the year of his grace—a celebration of God's destruction of our enemies—and to comfort all who mourn, to care for the needs of all who mourn in Zion, give them bouquets of roses instead of ashes, Messages of joy instead of news of doom, a praising heart instead of a languid spirit. Rename them "Oaks of Righteousness" planted by God to display his glory. They'll rebuild the old ruins, raise a new city out of the wreckage. They'll start over on the ruined cities, take the rubble left behind and make it new. You'll hire outsiders to herd your flocks and foreigners to work your fields, but you'll have the title "Priests of God," honored as ministers of our God. You'll feast on the bounty of nations; you'll bask in their glory."[3]

With this scriptural passage in mind, I have a solid sense of mission and calling to carry out a neighborhood transformation among uDAIs in New England. I am specifically concerned with how we can do all this beyond the church building's walls

---

3. Isa 61:1–7 (MSG).

within the context of my calling as a pastor in the church.[4] My daily preoccupying question has always been: "How can we as a church find our purpose?" To answer the question of what should be the church's purpose, my answer, of course, is that the church has to become involved in the neighborhood and begin the work of transformation there. The church has to be salt and light to the world around us, sweetening our neighborhood, preserving it. The church also has to be a pacesetter providing the pathway for the people in our neighborhood.[5]

Another scriptural passage that motivates me for this type of mission comes from Revelation 21, where verses 3–4, in particular, emphasize God's immanence within the neighborhood. The radical implication of this is that God has opted to stay with people in the neighborhood rather than to dwell in the many edifices built for him in contemporary times.[6] The central idea is that God is now resident in the neighborhood, ready to help men and women escape their pain and wipe away their tears. God has changed his location to the neighborhood, where the oppressed, the marginalized, and those who have their backs against the wall dwell. Neglecting this section of the larger society is neglecting God himself, because, he says, whatever you do to the least of these, it is me you are doing it to invariably.

> I saw Heaven and earth new-created. Gone the first Heaven, gone the first earth, gone the sea. I saw Holy Jerusalem, new-created, descending resplendent out of heaven, as ready for God as a bride for her husband. I heard a voice thunder from the throne: "Look! Look! God has moved into the neighborhood, making his home with men and women! They're his people, he's their God.

4. "Neighborhood" is understood as comprising more than the geographic space surrounding the church. Since African immigrants create their own social networks, it is that "neighborhood" that I hope to transform.

5. Matt 5:13–14 (KJV).

6. "Edifices" as used in this context is a metaphor for all kind of buildings called "churches" today. I do not doubt that God still works with people in those edifices as one of his lesser options of blessing people, but the most important fact is that God is now resident with people in the neighborhood.

He'll wipe every tear from their eyes. Death is gone for good—tears gone, crying gone, pain is gone—all the first order of things gone." The Enthroned continued, "Look! I'm making everything new. Write it all down—each word dependable and accurate.[7]

In my understanding, the church is not about building monuments such as cathedrals and lovely headquarter offices as some African community churches are doing today, but getting into the neighborhood and transforming lives. That is where the real action is and where the real needs are so obvious. God is interested in creating a brand-new world where the needs of the oppressed people of the society will be met and where he will be present with them until the new world order is created.

Furthermore, verses 21–27 vividly describe the context of that neighborhood; they say it is paved with gold, God and the Lamb bringing their light into it and becoming the Temple thereof, the earth's kings bringing their splendor into it, and its gates are never to be shut by day or night.

> The main street of the city was pure gold, translucent as glass. But there was no sign of a Temple, for the Lord God—the Sovereign-strong-and the Lamb are the Temple. The city doesn't need sun or moon for light. God's glory is its light, the Lamb its lamp! The nations will walk in its light and earth's kings bring in their splendor. Its gate will never be shut by day, and there won't be any night. They'll bring the glory and honor of the nations into the city. Nothing dirty or defiled will get into the city and no one who defiles or deceives. Only those whose names are written in the Lamb's Book of Life will get in.[8]

What will be a significant impact of my taking the mission into the neighborhood, and how does the vision of the New Jerusalem connect with the African immigrant "neighborhood"? I believe the passage above holds the key to that. There will be an utter transformation! The lives of men and women will be changed.

7. Rev 21:1–5 (MSG).
8. Rev 21:21–27 (MSG).

The African immigrant neighborhood's visible area will become a desirable place to live for everyone because the nobles and kings (the affluent citizens and top government personnel) will bring their honor and glory into it. The right and the dignity of every member of the neighborhood will be protected.

The idea of neighborhood transformation should be one of the marks of a true church. Feeding the hungry, quenching the thirst of the thirsty, and stopping the weeping, the pain, and mourning among our African immigrant neighbors is what I consider the hallmark of our Christian mission. Unfortunately, the church is failing in this mission, and because of this, people have resorted to seeking help elsewhere. What is the role of the church in all of these things? What should the churches be doing? What are the African churches in the diaspora doing to safeguard the situation?

Immanuel—God with Us

One of the most significant revelations of the Bible is the idea of God being with us, which the prophet Isaiah called "Immanuel," interpreted as "God with us."[9] God left the glory and splendor of heaven to come and dwell physically with men. He did not just reside with people but embodied their very nature by taking on human flesh and blood. In that sense, my notion of neighborhood transformation would take its bearing from what Mark R. Gornik and Maria Liu Wong express in their book *Stay in the City: How Christian Faith Is Flourishing in an Urban World.* They state that "the vocation of urban Christians begins with presence; it is a calling to be present with and open to God in the local context, attending to what is in front of us with all of our senses."[10] God is no longer in a distant place called heaven; he is right in the midst of the neighborhood embodied in the suffering masses within the community. The Word became flesh and blood and moved into

9. Isa 7:14; Matt 1:23 (KJV).

10. Gornik and Wong, *Stay in the City,* 6.

the neighborhood.[11] Gornik and Wong argue further that "ministry is theology on the ground, asking and answering questions of faith and life, work and home, love, and neighbor in a dynamic, constantly changing the urban world that we live in every day."[12] Ministry requires understanding and interacting with specific details of another person's life and, in this context, the undocumented immigrants' life. Each passing day of an undocumented immigrant is laden with many unanswered questions about their existential life and the desire to be treated as a bona fide human. The notion of God moving into the neighborhood is an idea that embraces the incarnational ministry of Jesus Christ as becoming flesh and blood to dwell among men and women to be with them, which Gornik and Wong describe as being "present with" or Wells depicts as "being with."

Samuel Wells, in his book A *Nazareth Manifesto: Being with God*, says that the most faithful form of Christian witness is "being with" others. Jesus himself demonstrated this example; he left the splendor of heaven to come to dwell in a stable—a building for livestock animals—to illustrate the lowliness of the kind of conditions in which some people often find themselves as poor, hungry, and marginalized citizens. Wells contrasts that mission to "working for," "working with," and "being for" others.[13] Wells argues that "being with" is both incarnationally faithful to the manifestation of God in Christ and depicts our anticipation eschatologically about the destiny of all things being in or with God.[14] Although Wells sees "being with" as a redundant state that offers no pragmatic solution. He emphasizes that empathizers in such a state cannot change the situation in most cases. He proposes to accompany people in such a situation to find their methods, answers, and approaches to dealing with their problems without losing their unique identities. The

---

11. John 1:14 (KJV).

12. Gornik and Wong, *Stay in the City*.

13. Wells, *Nazareth Manifesto*, 23.

14. Wells, *Nazareth Manifesto*, 23.

idea is to start with the people's assets and not their lack of them—just enjoying people for their own sake.[15]

In my case, I do not wish to only be "present with" uDAIs, as Gornik and Wong rightly suggest, or only adopt the mindset of "being with" them, as Wells argues. These dispositions are often not action oriented and may pass for a carefree attitude in my estimation. My struggles to become a legal resident in the U.S. has helped prepare me to assist uDAIs by "being with" them, being "present with" them, but also "working for" them, working with them, and "being for" them.

For instance, "being with" uDAIs means sharing in their plight and experiencing the full weight of what it means to be an aspiring legal resident, as in my case. It equally means providing resources and information that guarantee access to healthcare, educational, and legal systems. Lack of knowledge about these resources' availability is one of the obstacles to living a fulfilling life. "Working for" them would mean starting a non-profit organization that will directly address some of the plights of uDAIs in the U.S. I see myself combining all of these roles, having been in similar shoes, walking a similarly treacherous path.

Why Howard Thurman's Theology and Philosophy Is My Ideal Theological Vision

Howard Thurman was compelled to answer what religion has to say to the masses of men and women who live with their backs constantly against the wall. He referred to the poor, the disinherited, and the dispossessed, particularly the African Americans' fate in his time, whose social and racial problems persist even today. He was curious to find what our religion has to say to them. Thurman asserted that the search for an answer to this question is perhaps the most crucial religious quest of modern life.[16] Resolving the social

---

15. Wells, *Incarnational Mission*, 11- 12.

16. Thurman, *Jesus and the Disinherited*, 13. My choice of Howard Thurman's philosophy is because it is in line with my church tradition's ideal of caring for the oppressed and the vulnerable within our neighborhood.

plight and dislocation of the uDAI is fundamentally a religious, moral obligation that demands "being for" my neighbor.

Thurman's answer to those who have their back against a wall was found in his interpretation of the meaning of the religion of Jesus. He argued that it was essential to investigate the religion of Jesus within the context of his era and peoples and probe into his teaching content about the poor and underprivileged.[17] Thurman argued that "Jesus of Nazareth was a Jew of Palestine when he went about his father's business, announcing the acceptable year of the Lord."[18] He identified Jesus as a poor Jew, whose birth placed him with the great masses of men on earth. Thurman argued that the masses of people are poor.[19] But Thurman also argued that Jesus was a member of a minority group amidst a dominant and controlling group (the Roman Empire).[20] Here I find Thurman's theology, which defies the theological interpretation of the gospel by oppressors, especially the privileged class or race, and situates it among those with whom Jesus identified himself, as my ideal philosophy. Thurman's theology broke the norms of gospel interpretation, which seem to care less for the less-privileged classes. Thurman's reinterpretation of Jesus and his birth context radically favors the oppressed, the marginalized, and the disinherited.[21] Thurman's philosophical ideal animates my vocation to start a legitimate ministry for the suffering and marginalized strangers, especially uDAIs.

In New England, undocumented immigrants are being targeted by unfavorable policies from the U.S. Citizenship and Immigration Services (USCIS) through deliberate acts of discrimination that interfere with access to food, healthcare, and housing.[22] The challenges facing uDAIs are urgent and require active participation

17. Thurman, *Jesus and the Disinherited*, 15.

18. Thurman, *Jesus and the Disinherited*, 16.

19. Thurman, *Jesus and the Disinherited*, 17.

20. Thurman, *Jesus and the Disinherited*, 18.

21. Thurman, *Jesus and the Disinherited*, 15–18.

22. Francois, "Green Cards Only," https://thehill.com/opinion/immigration/459233-green-cards-only-for-immigrants-with-green.

from Christ's body, the church. African churches must be present with them in the midst of the challenges they face.

Thurman's radical theology changed the rules of how people should interpret the gospel; he stood in contrast to the prevailing interpretation of his day, where Scripture readings were guided by the privileged class and race. In like manner, we have chosen to identify with uDAIs in our church's context.[23] We want to position ourselves as a habitation of hope, a community for strangers. We are aware that Jesus Christ himself was a stranger in Egypt whose parents sought political asylum because of the unstable and hostile government in his home country. "And . . . an Angel of the Lord appeared to Joseph in a dream, saying 'Rise! Take the child and his mother with you and flee into Egypt, and stay there until I tell you, for Herod will look for the child to destroy him. And rising, he took the child and his mother that night and fled to Egypt."[24] It is possible for those who have the privilege of citizenship to read this scriptural passage without it conveying any critical meaning of the difficulties of migration and without genuinely understanding undocumented immigrants' lives. When the undocumented read this passage, it often connects them with the pain and hopelessness of being uprooted from once-familiar territory.

The radicalism of Christ's incarnation is not only about God coming down into the world to put on a fragile human body. But, most importantly, God choose to identify with Joseph and his family, who had fled the tyrannical rule of the empires. By his incarnational mission, as the Son of Man, Jesus embodied the plight of the oppressed and the disinherited when he walked on this earth. Jesus' family fled to Egypt to become political refugees because of Herod's brutally ruled regime. Herod had been empowered by a foreign colonial power in Rome to forcefully misrule the indigenous settlers of Galilee. Jesus' physical presence in Egypt invites us to ask why he should descend to that way of life. Herod had no other priority other than to ensure profits by taking taxes and remitting the same to the Roman headquarters unhindered. Herod,

---

23. Thurman, *Jesus and the Disinherited*, 14–18.
24. Matt 2:13–14 (KJV).

in particular, was benefiting greatly from this oppressive rule, like many elites within the Latin American countries today who sign trade agreements with the U.S. government that are detrimental to the continued survival of their citizens. The citizens have no other way of fighting back other than to migrate en masse into U.S. territory, where they believe they might at least have a share of the bounty that has been stolen from them.[25]

Jesus, a colonized man and a traveling stranger along with his parents by every standard, fit the perfect category of what we know today in our modern nationhood as undocumented immigrants. He could not be called an "undocumented immigrant" then because there was no such concept. He was more or less like a traveling sojourner desperately looking for where to live because of the reign of terror from the hand of Herod. Jesus together with his parents became sufferers of political injustice far beyond their own making and did not have a choice, other than to relocate to a neighboring country in Egypt. Therefore, in God's estimation, the responsibility toward aliens is so uppermost that God incarnated Godself as an alien. To ask why Jesus was in Egypt is to ask why there are undocumented immigrants in the U.S.[26]

Who Is My Neighbor?

Just then, a lawyer stood up to test Jesus. "Teacher," he said, "what must I do to inherit eternal life?" He said to him, "what is written in the law? What do you read there?" he answered, "you shall love the Lord your God with all your heart, and with all your soul, and with all your strength, and with all your mind; and your neighbor as yourself." And he said to him, "you have given the right answer; do this, and you will live." But wanting to justify himself, he asked Jesus, "And who is my neighbor?" Jesus replied, "A man was going down from Jerusalem to Jericho, and fell into the hands of robbers, who stripped him, beat him, and went away, leaving

25. De la Torre, U.S. Immigration Crisis, 154–56.
26. De la Torre, U.S. Immigration Crisis, 156.

him half dead. Now by chance, a priest was going down that road; and when he saw him, he passed by on the other side. So likewise, a Levite, when he came to the place and saw him, passed by on the other side. But a Samaritan while traveling came near him; and when he saw him, he was moved with pity. He went to him and bandaged his wounds, having poured oil and wine on them. Then he put him on his animal, brought him to an inn, and took care of him. The next day he took out two denarii, gave them to the innkeeper, and said, "take care of him; and when I come back, I will repay you whatever more you spend." Which of these three, do you think, was a neighbor to the man who fell into the hands of the robbers?" He said, "the one who showed him mercy." Jesus said to him, "Go and do likewise." [27]

To answer the question of the lawyer about who his neighbor was, Jesus needed to tell the story of the Good Samaritan above to illustrate his point. He recounted how God's ultimate plan for all humankind, regardless of the nation people come from, is to do the will of God by obeying the laws that will guarantee eternal life. The Good Samaritan was not an exception among the people living in Samaria because of his virtue. Instead, he was simply fulfilling what God's plan is for all people and nations. The man by the wayside was a traveler who was attacked on his way. He was a stranger to the Good Samaritan, who opted to help him out of his precarious situation despite their differing national identity. He wasn't the Good Samaritan nextdoor neighbor as we might want to assume. He was a traveling stranger turned into a neighbor. It is this similar understanding I have about uDAIs who were like traveling strangers which I hope to turn into neighbors within the African community in the New England neighborhood. It is fascinating that the people who had laws like the priest and the Levite failed to embody the rules in their daily life encounters. Instead, they chose to step onto the other side of the road, failing to meet the man that was robbed, beaten, and left half dead to go and fulfill their "religious" activities hastily.

27. Luke 10:25–37 (NRSV).

It is incredible that in our contemporary time, some religious men and women like the priest and Levite in this parable seem to be lost in their religiosity and, in most cases, lost in their devotion to church programs and activities. They fail to continue to extend God's mission to their neighbors whom they can see. They love their worship of God and religious ritual performances but shirk in fulfilling their charitable responsibilities toward such neighbors. The Parable of the Good Samaritan that Jesus told highlights another of Jesus' points about God's mission in Matthew 25:31–46, which I have referred to several times in this book. In this passage, Jesus acknowledges that those feeding the hungry and giving drink to the thirsty, welcoming strangers, clothing the naked, taking care of the sick, and visiting prisoners are making these gestures to him. Similarly, those who fail to do them are also doing the same to him. Therefore, we can infer from the passage that doing God's mission towards our neighbor shows care and concern towards God Himself. The lawyer had the whole thing mixed up at that point because he could not connect the dots between helping his neighbor and fulfilling God's law as the same obligation. He understood what his responsibilities toward God entailed. He, however, failed to understand that when he showed mercy to his neighbor, he was indirectly fulfilling the mission of God here on earth.

"Which of these three, do you think, was a neighbor to the man who fell into the hands of the robbers?" Jesus queried. The question still reverberates even in our contemporary time. Of course, the lawyer responded, "the one who showed him mercy." Jesus said to him, "Go and do likewise."[28] In this passage, the silent hero was the Good Samaritan, who, under his national identity, was supposed to be a despised Samarian citizen. The priest and the Levite could not even measure up to him. The Good Samaritan adopted God's laws that were primarily given to form the Israelites as a community of God's holy people and nation. He not only adopted them but also applied the same to his lived experience to perpetuate God's mission here on earth.

28. Luke 10:36–37 (KJV).

The command to "go and do likewise" by Jesus to that law-yer and us today continues to form people for mission. In my ministry, this command means a lot to me as l continue to extend God's mission among the uDAIs in New England. Unfortunately, many African churches in New England do not have a formidable ministry toward them despite the significant number of uDAIs in the region. At best, what most African churches are doing is similar to what the priest and Levite did in Luke 10:30–32. They occasionally criticize the conditions and what the uDAIs suffer but will not submit and work hard to release them from their pre-dicament and provide generous and authentic hospitality. They are extremely busy with church programs and activities. Many African churches have missed the ministry opportunities toward uDAIs, such as: feeding them, welcoming strangers, providing legal support and access to affordable healthcare, housing, and public education for immigrant children.

Other Sheep Not of This Fold

I want to emphasize that the work of neighborhood transforma-tion does not include only those who come to the church building. There are other sheep that Jesus claims are not of this fold that he is under obligation to bring into his kingdom. He does not just want to bring them into his fold casually, but he is determined to lay down his life for these sheep.[29] To capture this section's essence, I would like to retell Samuel Wells's story in his book *Incarnational Mission: Being with the World*.

There was this sweet old lady who was traveling on a train. She found a good seat in the train and settled down for the long ride. At the next stop, a young man in a business suit boarded the train and sat opposite the woman. The old lady brought out her Bible and began to read and meditate on what she was reading. The young man, out of curiosity, was surprised that someone was sitting op-posite him who was not preoccupied with a small electrical device.

29. John 10:14–18 (KJV).

The young man was curious to find out what she was reading. Realizing that it was a Bible, he asked skeptically, "Do you believe those stories?" The old lady replied without moving her head from her book, peering over her half-rimmed spectacles, "I most certainly do, young man." Unafraid, the man interrogated, "What about that old geezer who was swallowed by a fish? How could someone survive in a fish for three days?" "You're talking about the prophet Jonah, young man. I have no idea how that happened, but I look forward to asking Jonah about it when we meet in heaven one day." The young man thought he had boxed her to a corner this time. "Fair enough, but what if Jonah's not in heaven? What if Jonah went to hell?" "Well, then," answered the old lady, smiling sweetly, "you'll be able to ask him yourself, won't you?"[30]

This story is both funny and perfectly depicts the worldviews people have about the church and the modern world in our contemporary society today. Wells recognized the old lady as representing the perspective that a lot of Christians have about the church. He argues that the church is readily perceived as old, charming, behind the times, and ineffectual. On a positive note, he was quick to point out the ingenuity and the simplicity of the old lady's faith in the authority of the Scripture and her firm belief in the ultimate destiny of all believers in heaven and the damnation of unbelievers in hell. She was also not hesitant in talking even to antagonistic and disrespectful strangers about her convictions. On the contrary, the young man represents modern society—assertive, impatient and professional, with modest regard for orthodox Christian faith, seeing the church as a funny figure.[31] Wells writes that "the story's funny because we assume the old lady's weakness, and yet we see the way her simple faith in the eternal power of God exposes the bombast of the young man."[32]

Wells invites us to think more deeply about the notion of salvation, as illustrated in this story. He asks, "How can we think more

30. Wells, *Incarnational Mission*, 1–2.

31. Wells, *Incarnational Mission*, 2.

32. Wells, *Incarnational Mission*, 2.

helpfully about salvation?"[33] The story of the old lady and the young man is funny, but it also exposes the deep flaws inherent in the way many Christians go about the message of salvation.

Let us leave aside the surprise response from the older woman for a moment and talk about men and women who are out there but are strangers to the inherent good news of the gospel of Christ. Gospel misrepresentation may occur when some careless and inefficient Christians make the invitation unattractive. The invitation may also be rejected because certain people belong to other faiths or are agnostics.[34]

The inherent question here now is, how do we reconcile the determination of Jesus the Good Shepherd to bring them into his fold by laying his life down for them?[35] Here is why I feel motivated to take my ministry beyond the church's building walls and be involved in neighborhood transformation. I am motivated to go after the other sheep that are not of this fold. My job is not to change them; that is left for Jesus to do.[36] My job is to seek them out through the unconventional approach of reaching them in the neighborhood. That is what my church members intend to do with our mission to uDAIs. We are aware that many of those that need help and resources may also not have been regular churchgoers. Still, we recognize that they are the individuals of whom Jesus says that when we reach them with our humanitarian efforts, we have done the same to him. It is important to note that Jesus's mission is not complete until those other sheep find their way to the fold.[37] Wells argues that "salvation is not something Jesus tosses our way with a shrug of shoulders as if to say 'take it or leave it.' Salvation is what the Good Shepherd lays down his life to make possible and continues to offer everyone, every day, in every way, however little we may value or understand it."[38]

33. Wells, *Incarnational Mission*, 5.

34. Wells, *Incarnational Mission*, 6–7.

35. John 10:14–16 (KJV).

36. 1 Cor 5:17 (KJV).

37. Wells, *Incarnational Mission*, 7.

38. Wells, *Incarnational Mission*, 7.

Here is the final future statement that Jesus made concerning his other sheep that are yet to be part of his fold: "There shall be one fold, and one shepherd."[39] Wells says that is the joy of God's ultimate desire, the joy and the longing of heaven. That is the destiny of all sheep: to be one flock under one shepherd.[40]

The Samaritan Woman at Jacob's Well

Undocumented immigrants will not necessarily come to the church building during regular worship services to be transformed. Extending ministry to such people will require ingenuity from caring shepherds going after the sheep to seek them out in the neighborhood. Such was the type of ministry that Jesus extended to the Samaritan woman who came to draw water at Jacob's Well. The story is well illustrated in John 4:4–42. Jesus transformed the ordinary call of duty whereby the usual expectation that the needy and poor people would come to him on their initiative, by taking the initiative himself and approaching them as in the case of the Samaritan woman. Jesus on his way to Jerusalem chose to travel through Samaria, a city most Jews deliberately avoided because of cultural and religious grounds. However, he focused on fulfilling his incarnational ministry. He knew that to reach out to the Samaritan woman at Jacob's Well, he had to go out of his way and go after her intentionally.

The author of the book *Restorers of Hope: Reaching the Poor in Your Community with Church-Based Ministries that Work* identifies some of the barriers that churches would likely encounter when ministering to needy people using the neighborhood transformational model of the Samaritan woman. The first is the reluctance to go where they are because those territories or locations are unattractive and unfamiliar.[41]Many African churches refuse to go to where undocumented immigrants are because such a

---

39. John 10:16 (KJV).

40. Wells, *Incarnational Mission*, 7–8.

41. Sherman, *Restorers of Hope*, 121–22.

ministry would not add to the church's bottom line in terms of financial gain. Extending ministry to undocumented immigrants is an expensive ministry. Most African churches are not eager to participate in such a messy task because of the significant cost implication. However, in my congregation, we love the idea of neighborhood transformation and are setup for its implementation. We are ready to practically meet the needs of those who want such help. Jambres (real name redacted), one of the people I conversed with, rightly pointed out during our conversation that for churches to help immigrants that have become undocumented, they have to "meet the immigrants where they are. Have a committee in place that looks into the plight of immigrants. The church should know the recent things that are happening in the world of these immigrants . . ."[42] The real ministries are with those who are at the margin of life: the poor, the hungry, the naked, the sick, and the strangers in our neighborhood.

Sherman identified another thing Jesus did to the Samaritan woman—he chose to speak to her despite their religious, cultural, and gender differences. Historically, the Jews had a very strained relationship with the Samaritans because Samaritans were considered religious heretics and half-breeds. The Jews also had a general disdain for their cultural and religious practices.[43]

In my context, ministering to uDAIs will require crossing similar religious and cultural lines; the uDAIs who live in the U.S. exhibit a wide range of cultural and religious beliefs. The African continent has approximately fifty-four countries, and each country in its own right is both culturally and religiously diverse. My church will have to contend with such cultural and religious diversity as we plan to bring transformation into our neighborhood.

Another barrier observed by Sherman was the desire of Jesus to help the Samaritan woman despite his foreknowledge of the woman as a miserable sinner. Jesus knew that the woman had lived with five different husbands and lived with another who was not

---

42. Jambres (real name redacted) is one of the people I had conversation with who had a temporary stay in the U.S. with a student visa.

43. Sherman, *Restorers of Hope*, 122.

her husband before their meeting.[44] These were enough grounds to refuse help to the woman, but rather Jesus chose to reach out to this woman in her most crucial hour of need and perhaps because the woman also helped Jesus by giving him water.

Undocumented immigrants may become illegal aliens by deliberately overstaying the legal duration provided for on their visas, illegally forcing their way into their country of residence through deception, or may have even tried to go as far as falsifying records as Jessica did (real name redacted), the uDAI who brought a proposal to me to write an affidavit for her and her "arranged husband," which I referred to in chapter 1. Jesus did not cover up the Samaritan woman's sin; neither should I cover up the truth or lie for Jessica to facilitate her immigration.

By contrast, Jesus squared up and confronted her about it. Yet, he did not allow her sin to hinder his ministry toward her.[45] Sherman counseled that "we may legitimately acknowledge another's sin and exhort this person to change his/her behavior, but we must be careful that our judgments do not prevent us from reaching out."[46] With this view in mind, I will not treat undocumented immigrants on the premise of their sins but on the premise of a helpless, poor person for whom God left his throne in heaven to relieve their pain and dwell among them in the neighborhood.[47]

Another barrier that Jesus overcame was the barrier of personal inconvenience. Sherman tells us that Jesus was hungry, since his disciples went to buy food and had not yet returned. She also said that he was tired from his journey.[48] Summarily, she argued that these "internal" obstacles of hunger and weariness did not stop Jesus from extending his ministry to the woman.[49] If I must succeed in my ministry to undocumented immigrants, I must go beyond doing what is convenient in the ministry and serve sacrificially.

44. John 4:17–18 (KJV).
45. Sherman, *Restorers of Hope*, 122.
46. Sherman, *Restorers of Hope*, 123.
47. Rev 21:3–4 (MSG).
48. John 4:6, 8 (KJV).
49. Sherman, *Restorers of Hope*, 123.

Like Jesus, my personal needs and comfort must be sacrificed to meet the undocumented immigrants where they are.

The final significant barrier that Sherman observed was that Jesus overcame time pressure. She narrated how Jesus experienced a change in his initial plan though he had planned to go to Jerusalem. His ministry to the Samaritan woman at the well necessitated a shift in strategy, as the woman hurriedly ran into the village, urging people to come and see a man who told her all that she ever did. Unexpectedly, many people came along and listened to Jesus. They even begged him to stay on with them a little longer to hear him teach. Consequently, Jesus remained in Samaria for three days more, and many people believed in him. The vital point to note was that he was flexible with his time and was willing to reorganize his travel plans to address the needs of the Samaritan villagers.[50]

To conclude this chapter, I will restate the central idea of the chapter as concise as possible. A first vigorous attempt was made to survey my theological and biblical vision for neighborhood transformation. I examined Thurman's theology, Isaiah 61, and Revelation 21, which present for me the dynamics of how a transformed neighborhood can be attained. The theological and biblical vision was constructed through the notion of God's immanence as a pervading presence of God in the neighborhood that puts an end to all the weeping, wailing, and pains of the people. I also examined the doctrine of incarnational ministry of Jesus Christ, which Gornik and Wong called "present with" and Wells depicted as "being with." These two concepts are so powerful in demonstrating the compassion of God on humankind. They have similarly taught me personally to be more empathetic with our uDAIs neighbors. Although, I argued in the chapter that being "present with" or "being with" uDAIs can be less actionable because their capacities to move people toward a solution might be limited. The more productive version is to also "work with," "work for," and "be for" them.

---

50. Sherman, *Restorers of Hope*, 123.

Chapter 4

Community Building in American Society and the Inclusion of Strangers

Introduction

THIS CHAPTER WILL DWELL on the philosophical framework of community building. Community formation has been observed to be a desirable thing in every culture. Throughout human history, every people, nation, tongue, and tribe have all attempted to build community in the best possible ways that they know. But one is left to wonder why all those communities that have been built in human history have failed to stand the test of time. The number of killings through wars and other human-originated violence that has been staged across history and time have left little or nothing to desire among the communities that have ever been built by humankind.

In this chapter, I set the stage for unraveling the definition of the concept of community, before contextualizing it within the context of the Christian calling to build a community of strangers in a pluralistic society like the U.S. This theme is the primary subject matter in Roberto Esposito's book *Communitas: The Origin and Destiny of Community*, in Jean-Luc Nancy's *Inoperative Community*, as well as in Nils F. Schott's article in Blanton, Ward, and Hent De Vries's book *Paul and the Philosophers*.[1]After examining the philosophical angle of community formation, the chapter will take a look at how the community of Israel was formed in the Old Testament with the inclusivity of foreigners by referencing the cases of the Gibeonites. My primary concern is how American society can effectively build a community of strangers without necessarily excluding anyone from being part of the community.

What Is a Community?

Examining the notion of a community, I will focus on the definitions of Nancy and Esposito. But before I go into Nancy and Esposito's definitions, let me ask, at what point would it be appropriate to say, "We have no choice but to exclude because of the damage such prior inclusion is doing to this community," and would there ever be any justification for such exclusion? In his book *The Inoperative Community*, Nancy sheds light on that by arguing that, primarily, there is no common substance that defines a community. He argues that "communism can no longer be the unsurpassable horizon of our time."[2] The premise on which Nancy bases this argument are the events that led to the breakdown of the earliest communities that supposedly created the modern era.[3] Nancy says,

> Community (or communism) is what we are being called toward, or sent, as to our most. But it is not a "to come", it is not a future or final reality on the verge of fulfillment, pending only the delay imposed by an approach, as maturation or conquest. For if this were

1. Esposito, *Communitas*; Nancy and Fynsk, *Inoperative Community*; and Schott, "Love and Stick."

2. Nancy and Fynsk, *Inoperative Community*, 8. "Communism" as it is used here is used interchangeably with "community" by Nancy.

3. Nancy and Fynsk, *Inoperative Community*, 9.

the case, its reality would be mythic as would be the feasibility of its idea.[4]

The point is that community is very elusive: the moment people say they get it and have it made, then they have missed the most important point of it. Arguably, from a philosophical point of view, community is presumed; more often it is shaped by the power of our expectation of the sort of thing it should be. Therefore, the idea of establishing a community by what the members hold in common is a mere myth. When people conceive of the community as a desirable end, most of the time it only exists as a utopian image in the mind. Its conception is a myth and embarrassingly elusive in its pursuit. Nancy remarks that "community without community is to come, in the sense that it is always coming, endlessly, at the heart of every collectivity (because it never stops coming, it ceaselessly resists collectivity itself as much as it resists the individual)."[5]

For Nancy, his idea of the community means members of a community becoming vulnerable or exposed to one another. Community in this sense has no boundary or limit in its broad execution. But the question remains: at what point should people push back and say, "We have no choice but to exclude because of the constraint such prior inclusion is bringing into the community"? This is the question that every community throughout human history has battled sooner or later.

Similarly, Esposito, perplexed by the "commonality" that hold a community together, states that "the communalization of social relationships occurs if and insofar as the orientation of social behavior—whether in the individual case, on the average or in the idea type—is based on a sense of solidarity: the result of emotional or traditional attachments of participants."[6] In agreement with Esposito, it is right to say that most cultures define community by what people have in common as the basis for their association. But Esposito argues further that defining a community

4. Nancy and Fynsk, *Inoperative Community*, 71.
5. Nancy and Fynsk, *Inoperative Community*, 71.
6. Esposito, *Communitas*, 3.

by the members' commonality is not usually the end goal because almost instantaneously it will be discovered that what defines such community is what is not familiar to those community's members. What community members do in most cases is therefore exclude others, discriminate, and exhibit ugly xenophobic gestures.[7]

So, this notion of the community without a common substance makes me wonder how the United States intends to build a pluralistic society with the justification of excluding certain groups of people from everyday exposure that people are supposed to have toward one another. What type of pluralistic community does the United States want to build? Is it a welcoming community for everyone irrespective of race, creed, and faith, or is it a community that restricts certain nationals and their faith? The debate about the type of community that the U.S. wants is now more pertinent than ever before. During Trump's administration, the United States pronounced a visa ban of specific visa categories that could lead to permanent residency from the citizens of countries like Nigeria, Eritrea, Sudan, Tanzania, Kyrgyzstan, and Myanmar. The rationale for the action provided by Trump's administration was the failure of the six countries to meet U.S. security and information-sharing standards. The irony of this allegation is that a country like Nigeria and all the six countries listed above have never had any of their citizens prosecuted for carrying out a terror attack on the United States in the last ten years or more.[8]

Prior to this visa ban on the countries mentioned above, immediately after Trump assumed office in January 2017, he signed an executive order on January 27 that imposed restrictions of movement for seven Muslim countries, suspended all refugee admission for 120 days, and barred all Syrian refugees indefinitely. The six countries mentioned earlier were not originally part of these seven Muslim countries in the executive order ban. These were strategic moves by Trump's administration to curb the inflow of immigrants from these countries and completely halt immigration from Africa into the U.S. Donald Trump never hid his disdain for nationals

---

7. Esposito, *Communitas*, 3.

8. "US Travel Ban," https://www.bbc.com/news/wolrd-us-canada-51335011.

COMMUNITY BUILDING IN AMERICAN SOCIETY

from Islamic countries all over the world and Africa, with Nigeria as a specific target. Nigeria is the most populous black African country with about 53.5 percent Islamic devotees, and the country with the highest number of African immigrants in the U.S.[9]

The pluralistic society that the United States wanted to build under Trump's administration was a pluralistic society of exclusion, a community not in the sense that Nancy and Esposito understand it. Esposito, for instance, in defining the scope of a community, emphasizes that a community is supposed to be united by an "obligation" in the sense that we say "I owe you something" but not "you owe me something."[10] I therefore infer from Esposito's definition of community that a community should always seek what it will give to others and not what to get from them.

More recently, because of the new events that have unfolded, some ethical concerns have arisen that raise questions about the usefulness of undocumented immigrants in American society. For instance, in the wake of the global pandemic caused by the novel coronavirus, the undocumented that were previously unwanted in the country became essential workers overnight. During the last twelve months of Trump's administration, he grappled with the global coronavirus pandemic, SARS-CoV-2 (severe acute respiratory syndrome coronavirus 2) or simply COVID-19.

The pandemic resulted in many disappointments for the American citizenry and a high mortality rate. Despite colossal failures by the Trump administration, the news media and some politicians were generous enough to acknowledge that some undocumented workers were providing critical essential services to the American economy during the pandemic. These undocumented workers in some cases were sacrificing their lives to put food on the table for the American people, from farm work throughout all the distribution networks across the United States. This is just one sector among many others where the undocumented population functioned within society. Stay-at-home policies, the pre-eminent

---

9. Central Intelligence Agency, *World Factbook*; Migration Policy Institute, "Nigerian Diaspora."

10. Esposito, *Communitas*, 6.

strategy before vaccination deployed to curb the coronavirus's spread, prevented many Americans from going to work. However, undocumented workers, motivated by a need to survive financially, risked their lives during the hazardous pandemic to work in roles other Americans tended to avoid.

The big question remains: how can the United States build a pluralist community of strangers without excluding immigrants and other minorities from being part of that community? Due to the threat that an undocumented immigrant poses to others in the community, the situation unexpectedly forced the government to have an all-inclusive view of the country's immigrant situation, because an illegal immigrant when left without access to healthcare becomes a potential threat to all. But viewing undocumented immigrants as an equal threat is not the equality that immigrants require.

To reflect on one of the fundamental issues that Esposito wants us to contemplate about what binds members of the same community together, he interrogates, what is the *"thing"* that unites a community that we can say is familiar to them? Is it some positive "things"? Is it a right? Is it wealth or interest?[11] What can we say joins everyone in the United States of America together? To answer that question, let me at this point interrogate the nuances of the Trump administration on the "public charge" rule as a case in point.

Donald Trump's administration introduced the "public charge" rule to forcefully exclude some immigrants from the "commonwealth" of the country; the rule took effect on February 24, 2020. The purpose of the "public charge" rule is to empower the U.S. Citizenship and Immigration Services with the authority to deny issuance of green cards—the critical step on the path to citizenship—to people who have used a wide range of non-emergency welfare programs.[12] The argument raised by Ken Cuccinelli is that immigrants should demonstrate a high level of self-sufficiency to

11. Esposito, *Communitas*, 6.

12. Dinan, "Trump Enforces 'Public Charge' Rule," https://www.washingtontimes.com/news/2020/feb/.

enjoy inclusivity in the commonwealth of American society. If self-sufficiency is critical for being included, is not being included also critical for self-sufficiency? Roadblocks to self-sufficiency for *legal* immigrants are enormous, from general ineligibility for education loans in order to pursue a livable wage with vocational training, to the roadblocks to self-sufficiency for undocumented immigrants, like tuition inequity due to ineligibility for in-state tuition rates.[13] Self-sufficiency is hard enough in American society, but being an immigrant makes it even more difficult.

According to Stephen Dinan of the *Washington Times*, the Trump administration argued that "the vision of self-sufficient immigrants has been part of the American vision since colonial times and was explicitly written into law in 1882 when Congress banned any immigrants who were unable to take care of himself or herself [*sic*] without becoming a public charge."[14] Here the elevation of self-sufficiency as a critical step to the inclusivity of migrants into the commonwealth of the American people was emphasized. But the disaster of individualism pointed out by Esposito was again reinforced by the argument put forward by Ken Cuccinelli, the acting chief of USCIS and later the acting deputy secretary at the Department of Homeland Security under the Trump administration, who commented about Trump's "entrepreneurial spirit." Cuccinelli said, "we have a president who is determined enough to make self-sufficiency matter again in a meaningful way."[15] He said further that such a "kind of entrepreneurial mentality is natural for him."[16] Here communal solidarity that should include everyone is betrayed by the paradox of what Nancy refers to as human beings

13. "Undocumented Student Tuition," https://www.ncsl.org/research/education/undocumented-student-tuition-overview.aspx; "In-State Tuition and State Residency Requirements," https://www.finaid.org/otheraid/stateresidency.html.

14. "In-State Tuition and State Residency Requirements," https://www.finaid.org/otheraid/stateresidency.html.

15. Dinan, "Trump Enforces 'Public Charge' Rule," https://www.washingtontimes.com/news/2020/feb/.

16. Dinan, "Trump Enforces 'Public Charge' Rule," https://www.washingtontimes.com/news/2020/feb/.

as mere producers.[17] Nancy laments and describes this as a significant drawback of the modern era, and by itself signifies a community disruption. His proposed recovery approach is through the social framework of "communism," but even communism failed to deliver on its promises. However, placing production before the welfare of the members of the community is not the way to go either, in my estimation.

Now, if self-sufficiency is critical for being "included," why was there a readjustment of policy and bending of the rule by the USCIS within three weeks of the law being given assent by the Supreme Court? Initially, the "USCIS encouraged all those, including aliens, with symptoms that resemble coronavirus (COVID-19) (fever, cough, shortness of breath) to seek necessary medical treatment or preventive services." The agency states that "such treatment or preventive services will not negatively affect any alien as part of a future public charge analysis."[18] The argument became one where the virus, potentially a threat to all, requires us to unite to battle this common enemy. This is because if an alien is left untreated, it is not just his or her problem alone but a potential threat to all. Amy Kapczynski, a senior policy analyst with the American Civil Liberties Union and a Professor of Law at Yale Law School, offered: "if people are afraid to go to a hospital to respond to requests from public health officials, then they—and all of us—are at much greater risk."[19] The notion of "community" conceived by Nancy and Roberto is defined primarily by people's exposure or vulnerability to one another and not by what is not familiar to the community. It is a negative uniting factor.

Furthermore, Amy said, "we need to protect our communities by enabling everyone to seek care and to help in the response."[20]

17. Nancy, *Inoperative Community*, 3.

18. Madan, "Coronavirus Testing Won't Count," https://www.miamiherald.com/news/local/immigration/.

19. Madan, "Coronavirus Testing Won't Count," https://www.miamiherald.com/news/local/immigration/.

20. Madan, "Coronavirus Testing Won't Count," https://www.miamiherald.com/news/local/immigration/.

Monique O. Madan of the *Miami Herald* writes that "people who were sick were deemed a 'burden' to the U.S. and their health conditions were counted against them when applying for a green card."[21] She states the position of the USCIS by writing that part of the government's antagonistic approach to immigrants has changed since the advent of the coronavirus: "Any immigrant who gets tested for the virus will not be negatively impacted."[22]

Fear is what is now determining the type of policies that are put out there for public adherence. The power of fear is so pervasive that it is dominating the political arena. Anxiety may be deployed depending on the gain-and-loss ratio to include and exclude anyone from the community. During Trump's administration, the fear of the alien population, which is shaping the demography landscape, is what I believe occasioned the rhetoric of exclusion. Amazingly, due to the threat coronavirus poses to everyone, the fear of death is now used to include everyone, even those that are undocumented.[23] No wonder Esposito affirms that "it is death and not life that holds us within the horizon of the common."[24]

Esposito has performed an excellent job trying to trace the source and the root meaning of the term *communis* by citing an ancient and presumably original sense of its usage. He says *communis* means one "who shares an office, a burden or a task."[25] Community is about sharing the burden. It's about members of the same community embracing the vulnerability of one another. The acceptance of the shared experience that each one brings into the group is not about looking for what you can get from them. Esposito sums it up by saying that "*Communitas* is the totality of persons united not by 'property' but precisely by an obligation or a debt: not by an 'addition' but by a 'subtraction' by a lack, a limit

21. Madan, "Coronavirus Testing Won't Count," https://www.miamiherald.com/news/local/immigration/.

22. Madan, "Coronavirus Testing Won't Count," https://www.miamiherald.com/news/local/immigration/.

23. Esposito, *Communitas*, 20–27.

24. Esposito, *Communitas*, 121.

25. Esposito, *Communitas*, 6.

that is configured as an onus, or even as a defective modality for him who is 'affected,' unlike for him who is instead 'exempt' or 'exempted.'"[26] Esposito emphasizes that the notion of a community is united by an "obligation", in the sense that we say "I owe you something" but not "you owe me something."[27] Going by this submission, does the U.S. government owe the undocumented immigrants an "obligation"? Or does the government only seek to exploit them based on the need of the hour for the government? Yes, I believe that the government does owe the undocumented immigrants an obligation because the Bible admonished the Israelites not to oppress a stranger who resided in their land but treat them as a citizen would be treated.

> When an alien resides with you in your land, you shall not oppress the alien. The alien who resides with you shall be to you as the citizen among you; you shall love the alien as yourself, for you were aliens in the land of Egypt: I am the Lord your God.[28]

Community formation is a desirable end among all people and cultures, but the misfortune of individualism as identified by Esposito is its most significant obstacle. Leaders of communities must now transcend the rhetoric of triumph of individualism and accept the vulnerabilities of all the intended members of the group.[29] The community has no function except the function that we impose on it. The reason the USCIS could go back and forth on the "public charge" rule to exclude and to include within the space of three weeks is because of people's imposed function on the notion of community.[30]

The question might now be asked: how can a community without a community be realized, in the words of Nancy? Would building such a community ever be possible in this postmodern

---

26. Esposito, *Communitas*, 6.
27. Esposito, *Communitas*, 6.
28. Lev 19:33–34 (NRSV).
29. Esposito, *Communitas*, 1.
30. Esposito, *Communitas*, 71.

era? My short answer is that a community without a community is only attainable when we are not excluding anybody from the commonwealth. What it then means is that we are all now willing to embrace the vulnerability of one another and share in the burden of one another.

Foreigners and Community Building in the Old Testament:The Gibeonites' Story of Inclusivity

Firth in his book *Including the Stranger: Foreigners in the Former Prophets* employs the story of Rahab and the Gibeonites as his justification for the practice of inclusivity in Israel. He finds the story of Rahab to be straightforward, in the sense that mutual loyalty was visibly displayed between Rahab and the spies. I won't be using the story of Rahab in this book because she was an indigenous Canaanite whose people were dispossessed like the Native Americans.[31] My understanding is that you cannot include those who are native born to a particular territory, especially if they were originally dispossessed by invaders. That is how I see the story of Rahab deployed by Firth in his book. On the other end, the story of the Gibeonites took a different trajectory. Firth detects some ambiguities in the account of the Gibeonites, which are somewhat challenging to capture in translation. For instance, the ESV (UK) suggests that they acted with "cunning,"[32] something that Firth argues can be seen once the whole story has been read, not on first reading. It is said that they acted with *orma*, a noun that can indeed denote "craftily," but can also be expressed more positively to mean "prudence."[33] The pro-immigrant advocates may view the Gibeonites' move as prudent while the anti-immigrant proponents might view it as cunning or crafty.

The rest of Joshua 9 explores Israel's response once they realized they had been deceived, with some calling for capital

31. Josh 2:8–21 (KJV).
32. Josh 9:4 (KJV).
33. Firth, *Including the Stranger*, 30; Prov 1:4 (KJV).

punishment.[34] Although many were not in support of such calls, the elders' prevailing view was that they could not break the covenant they had made with the Gibeonites. When the Gibeonites were confronted with this allegation, they responded that they acted that way because of their fear of what Yahweh had commanded Moses to do to all the inhabitants of the land—that they should be destroyed.[35] The consensual agreement between the Israelites and the Gibeonites was for them to work in the sanctuary building for Israel by cutting wood and drawing water.[36]These were menial jobs but were significant enough to prevent them from being destroyed.[37] Firth opines that "they are cursed, but it is a curse that enables them to continue living in Israel."[38]

Negotiating exceptions for undocumented immigrants requires prudence and cunning. Similarly, one emphasis has been to appeal to the U.S. government to refrain from using inhuman punishment for arrested illegal aliens through harsh conditions in detention, forceful deportation, or separation from family members, particularly young children. Most undocumented immigrants will not compete for jobs with mainstream American citizens as some have alleged. As Lynda Gratton of the London Business School observed, reacting to the sentiment of a massive job loss in America and Europe due to immigration, "That is not true; job loss is due to automation."[39] The U.S. government can learn from Joshua and the elders of Israel by promoting the kind of consensual agreement between the Israelites and the Gibeonites (even if it will be unwritten). The Gibeonites were primarily engaged in constructing sanctuary buildings for Israel by cutting wood and drawing water,[40] and an argument remains that most undocumented immigrants do not even venture past the menial

34. Josh 9:20 (KJV).

35. Firth, *Including the Stranger*, 31.

36. Josh 9:27 (KJV).

37. Firth, *Including the Stranger*, 32.

38. Firth, *Including the Stranger*, 32.

39. Gratton, "Future of Work," http://bit.ly/2fQAmop.

40. Josh 9:27 (KJV).

jobs available, so long as they are paid and can put food on their table. However, an important point to note is that ensuring the inclusivity of the undocumented immigrants and the pluralistic vision of American society the way that Gibeonites achieved inclusion does entail some forms of exploitation. I will not focus on that in this chapter. The primary argument here is that for the pluralistic vision of American society to be authentic, it must be a vision of inclusivity of everyone without exception.

Excluding people from the community only leads to the loss of community in the truest sense of it, where there is no sense of responsibility toward one another. If the community is dissolved through exclusion, the loss becomes imminent. Nancy interrogates: what has the community lost? Nancy argues that it is "the immanence and the intimacy of communion."[41] This is the *munus* gift that Paul said should be used to benefit others, or the *communis* Esposito refers to as an office one shares, a burden, or a task.[42] Nancy rightly points out that the loss is only in the sense that such "loss" is immanent of community itself.[43] He posits that "Immanence, communal fusion, contains no other logic than that of the suicide of the community that is governed by it."[44] Nancy claims that "the unworking of community takes place around what Bataille for a very long time called the sacred, which he precisely labeled the unleashing of passions."[45] Summing it up, Nancy writes that "the presence of the other does not constitute a boundary that would limit the unleashing of 'my' passion: on the contrary, only exposition to the other unleashes my passions."[46] He states further that the community is the sacred, and it is the hallow stripped of the sacred. He says the sacred—the separated, the set-apart—no longer proves to be the expressive goal of an

41. Nancy, *Inoperative Community*, 12.

42. Esposito, *Communitas*, 6.

43. Nancy, *Inoperative Community*, 12.

44. Nancy, *Inoperative Community*, 12.

45. Nancy, *Inoperative Community*, 32.

46. Nancy, *Inoperative Community*, 32–33.

unrealistic communion but ideally made of nothing, other than the sharing of community.[47]

It is hoped that the coronavirus's effect might cause a massive loose end in future immigration policies since Americans and all immigrants regardless of legal status can all find common ground under the threat of the COVID-19 pandemic. Many uncertainties surround the prospect of uDAIs in the U.S. today. President Joe Biden's administration demonstrates sympathy for immigrants generally, and practically Biden has proposed an eight-year path to citizenship for the over thirteen million undocumented immigrants currently residing in the U.S. However, anxiety now remains concerning how the House and Senate will respond to Biden's proposal when it is brought to a vote.[48]

Yielding to the Calling of the Church as a Miniature Community in the New Testament

From the New Testament point of view, Nils F. Schott's argument begins with the opening verses of Paul's first letter to the church in Corinth. Schott refers to the theme that forms the epistle's crux, which is how to be a Christian proper: how to be a worthy follower of Christ. He discusses the call's idea—as the calling from God, and when one yields to the call, one becomes a missionary who has the responsibility of calling others to form a community. The community Schott says Paul is referring to here is the church.[49] Schott reads Paul as saying that his call can be accepted as a gift only when it is not received for oneself but handed on, given as a gift, and used for the benefit of others. For Paul, the difficulty lies in knowing what one is called to do. Schott here is reaffirming Nancy and Esposito's positions, both of whom see community as an obligation we give and not as a debt that somebody owes us.[50]

---

47. Nancy, *Inoperative Community*, 34–35.

48. Boak, "Biden Calls for Bipartisan Action," https://www.usnews.com/news/politics/articles/2021-07-02/biden-to-host-naturalization.

49. Schott, "Love and Stick," 310–11.

50. Schott Nils F., "Love and Stick," 311.

Here is where I see my calling to transform the neighborhood falling in line with Schott's notion of community building: I believe that this type of communal based community is mostly lacking in most of our modern communities today. I therefore feel a solid commitment to advance this in my neighborhood. I will discuss more on this in chapter 6, which deals with the incarnational outreach of my church.

The main talking point in this chapter is that as much as a community is a desirable end in every culture, what we have found out is that it is very evasive. When people say they understand, they usually end up missing out on the most important point about it. Because according to Esposito and Nancy, the community is not about sharing common values but embracing one another's vulnerabilities.

This book's chapter has demonstrated how the COVID-19 pandemic forced the U.S. to shift its definition of who is to be included in the commonwealth, even if it is going to be temporary because of the potential threat of the virus. The U.S. government allowed undocumented immigrants to get free COVID-19 testing and treatment if they suspect that they have the virus without any punishment or consequences. Undocumented immigrants were allowed to enjoy these free services because when they are left untreated of the virus, they become a potential threat to all of us. In sum, this chapter reminds us of what every community has to grapple with either sooner or later: at what point can we say we have no choice but to exclude because of the constraint such inclusion is bringing into the community?

Chapter 5

Theological and Biblical Resources for Congregational Practice of Hospitality

Introduction

THIS CHAPTER WILL FIRST examine the theology of hospitality by exploring its meaning. Subsequently, an effort will be made to focus on one of the core principles of community formation: hospitality practices.

The chapter will discuss a biblical basis for hospitality as a model approach for treating strangers, including citing relevant examples from the Hebrew Bible.[1] The risk and shortcomings of Hebrew scriptural practices of hospitality require modification to fit a contemporary theology of hospitality. What the Bible has to say about hospitality will be traced throughout the Bible and explained, followed by a treatment of some sermon and Bible study topics to aid a robust understanding of the subject matter.

---

1. The biblical practices will be read through the lens of Anglican traditions, and it will guide the understanding of hospitality throughout the thesis. My identity as an Anglican priest also shapes my reading of various texts.

The Theology of Hospitality

Hospitality as a concept has an undertone that is easier said than practiced. Jayme Reaves counsels, in his book *Safeguarding the Stranger: An Abrahamic Theology and Ethic of Protective Hospitality*, that instead of establishing a definition of hospitality, it is more helpful to inquire into the meaning of hospitality.[2] He argues that hospitality is about the ideas of welcome and openness to others. He observes that what is tricky here is defining the full extent of welcome and openness.[3] Reaves also raises other concerns, such as whether hospitality is simply the act of welcoming our inner circle members or welcoming all others that are distinctively different from us. He says it is easier to welcome people like ourselves but harder to accommodate the others who are not like us. Therefore, Reaves wants to investigate what openness consists of and how people should practice it. There are other related questions regarding the notion of space and its mastery that Reaves wants us to ponder, such as what the experience of a shared space would look like in each person's context. He is interested in determining the difference between genuine hospitality and superficial hospitality. He wants to know the boundaries of operation of such genuine or superficial hospitalities and to whom they should be extended.[4] These are the primary concerns of Reaves as far as understanding what hospitality means in practice.

There are other conceptual meanings of hospitality by other scholars, some of which I will also consider in this section. Marlea Gilbert, in her article "Hospitality in Sacred Space," sees hospitality as the welcoming of friends and strangers in the name of God. The definition by Gilbert is perhaps what is most expected from people of faith especially Christians. As expected, Gilbert holds the view of hospitality as a fundamental part of Christian faith practice, which has its origin in the Hebrew Bible. She suggests that as a congregational practice, it must not be left in the hands of a selected few

2. Reaves, *Safeguarding the Stranger*, 49.
3. Reaves, *Safeguarding the Stranger*, 49.
4. Reaves, *Safeguarding the Stranger*, 49.

who signed up as greeters welcoming visitors into the church, but a shared practice among all believing Christians.[5] Letty Russell, in her book *Just Hospitality: God's Welcome in a World of Difference*, echoes the same sentiment by stating that "hospitality is not optional for Christians, nor is it limited to those who are specially gifted for it. It is instead a necessary practice in the community of faith."[6] She argues that hospitality in most cases requires reaching across individual differences and going beyond the bounds of our comfort to bring the love of God to the others. Russell beautifully brings it home by stating that "hospitality is the practice of God's actions to bring justice and healing in our society."[7]

As a human species, humankind craves a just and equitable society where the love of God is a shared experience among people regardless of their differences. However, it must be emphasized that justice and healing in the society can only be established when Christians are attentive to the needs of the poor and the marginalized around them. As Mary Anderson suggests, Christians must be constantly reminded that the purpose of hospitality, theologically speaking, is to prepare a welcoming space for encounters with God's word for communal participation and attentive listening. The onus is on Christians to create such a spatial openness where everyone in the church will be attentive to the needs of the people as they hear the word of God.[8] Christians cannot effectively bring justice and healing to strangers, especially the undocumented immigrants in their neighborhood, if they are not paying attention to what the undocumented immigrants need or providing a welcoming space to hear them out.

But as human social interaction continues to evolve with different dynamics and varying degrees of complexities, hospitality as a virtue in public and private life has been subject to severe scrutiny, especially in our contemporary time. Communities all over the world are beginning to exhibit what Arthur Sutherland

5. Gilbert, "Hospitality in Sacred Space," 21.

6. Russell, *Just Hospitality*, 18.

7. Russell, *Just Hospitality*, 19.

8. Anderson, "Hospitality Theology," 643.

refers to as "compassion fatigue" in his book *I Was a Stranger: A Christian Theology of Hospitality.*[9] Americans are encountering strangers with increasing suspicion at every nook and cranny of society. The September 11 terrorist attack and the Boston Marathon bomb explosion of 2013 are two events that exacerbated the fear that Americans express concerning strangers. Good American citizens still welcome strangers, but many people are instead very suspicious. Occasional disruption of a genuine show of hospitality should not cause Americans to rescind their good gestures towards strangers. Hence, Russell challenges our local, national, and global institutions to practice hospitality with justice by overcoming our struggles and fear of difference and to break all the barriers that still keep us apart.[10]

The election that brought Donald Trump to the Presidency is a clear testament to the limits of American hospitality. I have previously stated how President Trump's administration directed its full wrath toward immigrants, primarily immigrants from Islamic countries and some African countries. But the U.S. government cannot continue to move in such a xenophobic direction and expect to build a healthy society. For the sake of peaceful co-existence, something drastic ought to be done to correct the abnormality and the general ill will directed toward strangers.

My argument then is to continue to emphasize that the practice of hospitality has been a valuable part of our Christian tradition that dates back to the time of Abraham in the Hebrew Bible and to the time of first-century Christians. Martin therefore, in his article "Old Testament Foundations for Christian Hospitality," challenges Christians to recapture hospitality as a vital and effective means of manifesting the love of Christ in the world.[11] To this end, I will ground the notion of being present with our stranger-neighbors (who have become undocumented) or being attentive to their needs within biblical traditions of hospitality. I am aware that no two immigration cases will occur exactly in

9. Sutherland, *I Was a Stranger*, 10.

10. Russell, *Just Hospitality*, 117.

11. Martin, "Old Testament Foundations," 1.

the same manner. But then I feel very strongly that my church should give generously to each African immigrant, irrespective of the nature of their claims, reasons for migrating, or legal status. Hospitality as a ministry model in my context will encompass how uDAIs can navigate the healthcare system, public education for their children, and immigration advisors.

The Bible contains countless injunctions for us to show hospitality to strangers in our neighborhood. Hospitality is one of God's particular commandments to Israel to help strangers because they were once in such a dilemma themselves in Egypt. Miguel De La Torre identifies three biblical grounds on which the treatment of aliens should be based.

1. The Jews were once aliens who were oppressed by the Egyptians.[12]

2. God always sides with and intervenes to liberate the disinherited.[13]

3. God's covenant with Israel is for everyone in the community to benefit, whether they are Jews or not.[14]

Martin, lending further voice to the practice of hospitality, argues that "in the context of increasingly pluralistic, multi-faith societies, it is necessary to construct new and effective paradigms for hospitality. Many communities are now populated with citizens who have little in common with one another, and each is suspicious of the other."[15] He asserts that "within these potentially adversarial contexts, the Christian community can serve as host to the "other" as a model of God's love to the world."[16] These biblical antecedents of hospitality suggest a paradigm for responding to the needs of the uDAIs within my neighborhood by demonstrating brotherly love and kindness to them.

---

12. Exod 22:21 (KJV).
13. Exod 23:9 (KJV).
14. De la Torre, *U.S. Immigration Crisis*, 154; Deut 26:11 (KJV).
15. Martin, "Old Testament Foundations," 1.
16. Martin, "Old Testament Foundations," 1.

A Compassionate God

God is a compassionate God. The implication of this is that God has chosen to be God-with-us. Henri Nouwen asserts that for us to feel the total weight of this divine solidarity, we should explore the experience of someone being with us. He says this will offer us a glimpse of what we mean when we say that God is a God-with-us. A God who came to share our lives in solidarity with all the mess, confusion, and unanswered questions that permeate our entire lives is the exact meaning of God taking on human flesh. As soon as we profess that God is with us, we have entered into a new realm of intimacy where God shares in our joys and pains, extending protection to us and suffering all of life with us.

In contrast to this, Nouwen states that "our whole sense of self is dependent upon the way we compare ourselves with others and upon the differences, we can identify. It is by our differences, distinctions that we are recognized, honored, rejected, or despised."[17] He argues further that the inclination for competition that often reaches the minutest recesses of our relationship prevents us from entering into full solidarity with each other, standing in the way of being compassionate.[18] So to be human in the true sense is to be hospitable; God has shown us an example by taking upon himself the very nature of humanity, showing his solidarity and compassionate love to all humankind. The exact point of Jesus coming into the world is to be with us.

Hospitality should be a sacrificial giving that Christians should offer to someone in distress without holding back. That is why the Bible admonishes us to "show hospitality to one another without grumbling."[19] Society cannot wait until people are badly injured through our competitive spirit before showing compassion or displaying our hospitability to them. We must rise above the petty concern of what is in it for us and fully manifest the love of Christ. The writer of Hebrews states, "do not neglect to do good and share

---

17. Nouwen, *Compassion*, 17.

18. Nouwen, *Compassion*, 17–18.

19. 1 Pet 4:9 (ESV).

what you have, for such sacrifices are pleasing to God."[20] We must share in the vulnerabilities of others by willingly offering to make sacrifices even when it is not convenient. Hospitality is not simply giving but also giving up our comfort zone.

Hospitality in the Old Testament

The most conspicuous story about hospitality in the Old Testament is the story of Abraham and his purported encounter with the three men who have sometimes been regarded as angels. The writer of Hebrews may have also alluded to Abraham's encounter, thus admonishing his hearer not to be forgetful to entertain strangers: for some have entertained angels unaware by doing so.[21] Angelic visitation was a frequent occurrence in the Old Testament. That was why the early patriarchs took it upon themselves to be a welcoming host to all and sundry, because they did not want to miss out on the great care that should be shown to an angel. The story of Lot and his visiting guests, who also turned out to be angels, also comes to mind.

Lee Roy Martin, whose work I am going to dwell on extensively in the next few pages, argues that hospitality was necessary for nomadic people because hotels were scarce in the wilderness in those days. The same argument could also hold for towns and cities, where inns were often non-existent.[22] We may want to ask, was hospitality freely offered to everyone in the ancient past? In response, Martin notes that people did not always offer hospitality to everyone in ancient times. The simple reason is that the traveler or a small group of travelers could be exposed to the peril of robbers and hostile tribes. Hospitality for the host could be dangerous as well, especially from the activities of traders and marauders, who are often without a home base and always viewed with suspicion. Marauders are wanderers who move across the land, hoping to

20. Heb 13:16 (ESV).
21. Heb 13:2 (KJV).
22. Martin, "Old Testament Foundations," 2.

take advantage of every opportunity to plunder and destroy weaker ones. Martin observes that hospitality in the Old Testament is sometimes misunderstood as kindness offered to the "stranger." He argued that was not always the case.

Although in the modern English language a "stranger" can simply mean a person or thing that is unknown or with whom one is unacquainted, in the Hebrew Bible the term is used more specifically to describe a sojourner or resident alien. So, a stranger is not a potentially dangerous traveler as much as a person from *without* who has chosen to stay *within* the community, one willing and ready to take up residence on a more or less permanent basis. The implication is that the stranger may not be unknown but might be a neighbor or friend and would not be viewed as a potential threat.[23]

Martin writes that the stranger, or resident alien, is not required to worship Yahweh or under any obligation to perform the ritual commands, but must subscribe to other laws like the one connected to labor on the Sabbath. The stranger must not be oppressed or exploited by the Israelites but should be protected by the law under the Mosaic covenant.[24]

Hospitality as a Provision for Shelter

Martin observes that Abraham's act of hospitality did *not* present an opportunity to offer protection for his guests, unlike the other biblical stories, where we find this element deeply enshrined in the narrative.[25] Two biblical examples that come to mind are the Lot stories as well as another from Judges 19. The men of Sodom wanted to violate Lot's three guests sexually. Still, Lot acted swiftly to cover for them and offered his daughters instead to satisfy

---

23. Martin, "Old Testament Foundations" 2.

24. Martin, "Old Testament Foundations," 2–3; Exod 22:21 (KJV), 23:9 (KJV); Num 9:14 (KJV), 15:15 (KJV); Deut 1:16 (KJV); 24:17 (KJV).

25. Martin, "Old Testament Foundations," 5.

their sexual urges.[26] The outcome was God's judgment on Sodom and Gomorrah.

The second example is in Judges 19, which is the story of a Levite and his concubine who lodged in the house of an older man in Gibeah. On the night of their arrival in the older man's house, the city's men surrounded the house and demanded that the older man turn over the Levite to them. But the older man would not accede to their request but instead persuaded them to have the Levite's concubine and his daughter instead. Although the city's men spared his daughter, unfortunately, the Levite's concubine was violated and abused sexually, leading to her eventual death. Martin states that in this ancient time, hospitality law did not protect women to the same extent that men were shielded. Questions are being raised by many modern readers in connection to this gender inequality. They therefore offer some caution about the way such texts are to be applied to contemporary contexts.

The Peril of Hospitality

Martin argues that safety concerns are legitimate not only in contemporary times but were also in ancient times. He asks, was everyone who appeared as a needy traveler in ancient times a harmless person? To this he remarks that some travelers conducted themselves deceptively to gain or take advantage of their host.[27] We have an example of the peril of hospitality from the Gibeonites, whom the Bible suggested acted with cunning behavior in Joshua 9 by their interactions with the Israelites· Although the Gibeonites did not pose an immediate potential risk to the Israelites, the deceptive approach with which they gained the attention of their host provides a ground upon which we can expect certain travelers with sinister motives to want to gain an advantage over their host. As much as this was true in ancient

26. Gen 19:8 (KJV).
27. Martin, "Old Testament Foundations, "5.

times, we are even more susceptible to such acts and expect it to happen in our contemporary communities today.

The Limitations of the Old Testament Hospitality Practice

Martin argues that as much as the Old Testament practice of hospitality is relevant to our contemporary situation, Christians should do away with some aspects of the procedure to fit the model into modern practice. Martin observed certain shortcomings in the Old Testament practice.

The first is the limited choice of travelling guests often accorded hospitality and only for a short period. Martin argues that there is a need to expand our notion of hospitality practice to accommodate all kinds of neighbors, especially those unlike us.[28]

Second, the choice of guests often excluded aliens and foreigners. We find a related example in the story of the Levite in Judges 19, where the traveling Levite was not favorably disposed to spend the night with the Jebusite because it was not an Israelite city and might be dangerous to pass the night in such an unfamiliar place. Instead, he diligently sought for a man who was not different from himself to spend the night.[29] As America aims to build a pluralistic society, our notion of inclusivity must without exception include people of all creeds, races, religions, and nationalities to create a flourishing community.

Another shortcoming of the Old Testament practice of hospitality is that it represented a more patriarchal tradition. The men were the ones who always decided which traveler would benefit from hospitality. The women, in most cases, were either ostracized or abused in the worst-case scenario.[30]

Finally, the Old Testament practice of hospitality was very limited in its goals because it only met the traveler's basic human

---

28. Martin, "Old Testament Foundations," 5.
29. Martin, "Old Testament Foundations," 6.
30. Martin, "Old Testament Foundations," 6.

needs like food, shelter, and protection. While this may have been essential for a traveler's survival, it was necessary to note that Christians must offer hospitality in more pertinent and innovative ways in today's world. Of course, this may include clothing, transportation, direct community participation, vocational education, and much more.[31] Although the Old Testament practice of hospitality can contribute to our understanding of hospitality, its limited practice is insufficient to provide the entire map to build a contemporary church practice. Hence, we must develop a more robust form of hospitality that is all-encompassing in our modern society. Our next goal will be building a contemporary theological understanding of hospitality where those limitations identified above will be effectively addressed.

Towards a Contemporary Theology of Hospitality

Martin identifies the fear of the difference between us and others as a significant hindrance to forging a hospitable relationship. He argues that these differences manifest in various forms, such as differences in language, customs, culture, religion, and race. He posits that these differences create barriers to understanding and that lack of understanding hinders the required bonding in relationships.[32]

To favor a move toward a contemporary theology of hospitality, Martin wants us to focus on our similarities first of all and then on our diversities as humans. He argues that our commonalities can bring us to a place of mutual sharing of *koinonia*, where we share deep fellowship. Then, of course, our differences can make our relationships more fascinating, exhilarating, and therapeutic; the diversities bring the uniqueness of the group members to bear and provide us with the missing links in our shared values. He suggests four major shared human traits that undergird a broadened contemporary theology of hospitality. They are: 1) "All Humans

---

31. Martin, "Old Testament Foundations," 6.
32. Martin, "Old Testament Foundations," 6.

Are Made in the Image of God"; 2) "All Humans as Relational Creatures"; 3) "All Humans as Dependent upon Each Other"; 4) All Humans as Travelers Hosted by God."[33]

All Humans Are Made in the Image of God

The fact that all humans are created in the image of God is the substantial ground on which the demonstration of hospitality to all kinds of people should be based. Martin suggests that we may differ in appearance and culture, but such differences are very limited.[34] Human beings are expected to be treated with honor and dignity because we are all a reflection of the image of God. Little wonder Jesus reiterated that "whatever you do to least of this my brethren, it is me you have done it to."[35] As much as God forbade us to make any graven image that will be like him, he graciously put his image into humankind. So, if we desire to show him love and serve him, we must do this by loving and serving our fellow human beings because humanity is the expression of God's image.

All Humans as Relational Creatures

Martin writes that the purpose of creating humanity was for a relationship, social interaction, and community. For this purpose, we should all strive for every human to enjoy the benefit of this relational need. At the outset of creation, God declared that "it is not good for man to be alone."[36] Martin suggests that our hospitality model should address the "aloneness" often experienced by the marginalized and oppressed people around us. He also believes that the relationship engendered by hospitality produces shared benefits between the giver and receiver of hospitality.[37]

33. Martin, "Old Testament Foundations," 6.
34. Martin, "Old Testament Foundations," 6.
35. Matt 25:40.
36. Gen 2:18 (KJV).
37. Martin, "Old Testament Foundations," 6–7.

All Humans as Dependent upon Each Other

Martin writes that beyond community formation, humans depend upon one another in a variety of ways.[38] He argues that the Old Testament recognizes our mutual dependency on one another and urges the stronger members of the community to support the weaker members: orphans, widows, resident aliens, the sick, the poor, the needy, and the vulnerable.[39] Martin says that the Old Testament imposes substantial penalties for oppressing the weak. Again, beyond the specific categories of dependent persons mentioned, the Bible generally echoes that humans depend heavily on each other and upon God.[40] In our contemporary society, we are dependent upon thousands of other people for our daily sustainability. We are not all the same in the area of our giftedness. The farmers among us provide food for us to eat because they need the money to meet their personal financial needs like sending their children to school, paying for utilities, etc. The business owners are dependent on the purchasing power of the buyers to continue to be relevant in business. It is a whole web of interconnectivity that each of us benefits from in one way or another. The idea of self-sufficiency is not sustainable in the long period of time when we consider the magnitude of interdependency that we all need as humans to survive.[41]

All Humans as Travelers Hosted by God

Martin suggested that if the purpose of hospitality is to nourish and provide protection for travelers who find themselves in a hostile land, then we all need hospitality because, to some extent, we are all like travelers out of place but hosted by God. The Bible regarded all of us as pilgrims traveling through the alien land enjoying the hospitality extended to us by God because of

38. Martin, "Old Testament Foundations," 7.

39. Martin, "Old Testament Foundations," 7.

40. Martin, "Old Testament Foundations," 7.

41. Martin, "Old Testament Foundations," 7.

his ownership of all creation.[42] Therefore just as God hosted us and accommodated us with the beautiful things of creation and did not discriminate against any of us based on our skin color, religious affiliation, cultural background, creed, or belief, we are supposed to extend the same goodness to others.

Congregational Practices of Hospitality

Given the crisis facing uDAIs as fully described in chapter 1 of this book, in this section I will seek to link the various theologies of hospitality already discussed with congregational practices to help my congregation grow in grace by providing holistic assistance to uDAIs. The first steps will be combining preaching sermons on biblical traditions of hospitality and organizing a series of Bible studies around the theme. I will set up an action reflection group to discuss the texts and how they relate to their lives, which I will then develop into sermons based on what they have discovered. Hopefully, the feedback loop methodology will enable me to broaden my congregation's horizon toward a holistic view of salvation that includes societal transformation, as seen in our ministry with African immigrants.

The overall purpose of congregational formation through sermons and Bible studies is to help my congregants understand biblical practices of hospitality as part of their duties as Christians. The following sermon topics and Bible studies will be listed and expounded upon to form my congregation for mission and societal transformation:

What Does the Bible Say about Christian Hospitality?

At least thirty different passages in the Bible directly relate to the subject of hospitality toward strangers. I would love my congregation to be informed about the usefulness of these scriptures and adopt them. Biblical practices of hospitality represent our

---

42. Martin, "Old Testament Foundations," 7.

Christian values and virtues. The most crucial step for me is to treat these scriptures first as texts to inspire enriching discussion about biblical hospitality by the church's action reflection group. I will later develop them into various sermon topics so that members of my congregation can continue to grow in grace. I will reference each of the scriptures and explain what they could mean in my church context.

1. "Do not neglect to show hospitality to strangers, for thereby some have entertained angels unawares."[43] The Bible does not want us to claim ignorance for the lack of hospitality shown to strangers, especially those who have decided to take a temporary or permanent residency within our community. Christians should treat them as though they are entertaining angels because angels are known to be conveyors of goodness. Since we do not know who might be carrying blessings to us, it is essential to treat everyone who crosses our path well.

2. "Show hospitality to one another without grumbling."[44] God does not want Christians to feel burdened or under coercion before being motivated to do well to others. Hospitality as a practice should be as natural to us as the air we breathe. It should be freely given without the expectation of direct reciprocity from the beneficiaries.

3. "Contribute to the needs of the saints and seek to show hospitality."[45] One of the noblest New Testament practices is hospitality. The book of the Acts of the Apostles dwells on this biblical practice so much that the disciples were often involved in bringing the proceeds of their properties to the apostles' feet for communal sharing. After consulting with James, Cephas, and John, those esteemed to be pillars regarding their ministry to the gentiles, the apostle Paul and Barnabas, were advised to continue in the grace bestowed on them by God. They were to remember the needy and the

43. Heb 13:2 (ESV).
44. 1 Pet 4:9 (ESV).
45. Rom 12:13 (ESV).

poor among their gentile converts in the daily ministration—
a practice that Paul affirmed they were already doing.[46] While
it is appropriate to think of the Old Testament hospitality as
being more inclusive, the New Testament scriptures speak
largely to the members of the household of faith, which
might imply the exclusion of certain people. However, that is
not my priority here, focusing only on the household of faith,
but on those who are desperately in need of our help.

4. "You shall treat the stranger who sojourns with you as the
native among you, and you shall love him as yourself, for
you were strangers in the land of Egypt; I am the Lord your
God."[47] As far as I am concerned, this scripture is an essential
verse about how strangers should be treated in the U.S. with
all working together to build a pluralistic society. Strangers
should not be treated with a different set of rules that dehu-
manizes them from the native-born in the land (the citizens).

5. . . . Appoint elders in every town, as I directed you . . . for an
overseer, as God's steward must be above reproach. He must
not be arrogant or quick-tempered or a drunkard or violent
or greedy for gain, but hospitable, a lover of good, self-
controlled, upright, holy, and disciplined."[48] This scripture
mainly speaks to those in leadership, especially those who
make policies to be hospitable and be a lover of the good. The
scriptures also speak to leadership at the congregational level
to establish a platform for doing good things among needy
people, especially, to the strangers among us.

6. "Whoever speaks, as one who speaks oracles of God; whoever serves, as one who serves by the strength that God sup-
plies—so that in everything God may be glorified through
Jesus Christ. To him belong glory and dominion forever and
ever. Amen."[49] The main thing here is as Christians set out

46. Gal 2:9–10 (ESV).

47. Lev 19:34 (ESV).

48. Titus 1:5,7–8 (ESV); 1 Tim 3:2 (ESV).

49. 1 Pet 4:11 (ESV).

to serve others within their neighborhood, they must be reminded that it is God who supplied the strength with which they are executing the good deeds done unto others. The motivation to will action and to execute it did not originally emanate from them but God. They must deeply appreciate and acknowledge that fact.

7. "And having a reputation for good works: if she has brought up children, has shown hospitality, has washed the feet of the saints, has cared for the afflicted, and has devoted herself to every good work."[50] This scripture refers to specific Christian duties that every responsible woman ought to carry out in the church in connection to good works and demonstration of hospitality. The command for hospitality is not a regulation set in stone for women only; it is equally demanded from their male counterparts. The act of feet-washing was widely practiced in ancient Israel for strangers, sojourners, or travelers. Jesus demonstrated humble service to others by washing his disciples' feet and counseled them to do the same.

8. "One day, Elisha went on to Shunem, where a wealthy woman lived, who urged him to eat some food. So, whenever he passed that way, he would turn in there to eat food."[51] As the Shunamite woman often welcomed Elisha into her home with very decent accommodation and sumptuous meals, we also, as Christ-followers, are expected to care for the strangers that come through our church's door with shelter and feeding when necessary.

9. "Beloved, it is a faithful thing you do in all your efforts for these brothers, strangers as they are."[52] Here John was commending his children in the Lord in one of the congregations that he helped to nurture into maturity for their good deeds toward their fellow brothers who were strangers among them. John's joy was beyond human comprehension and

50. John 13:14–17 (ESV).
51. 2 Kgs 4:8 (ESV).
52. 3 John 1:5 (ESV).

description but was worth the glorification of God—that is a praise to God.

10. "And after she was baptized, and her household as well, she urged us, saying, 'If you have judged me to be faithful to the Lord, come to my house and stay.' And she prevailed upon us."[53] Lydia was a wealthy merchant and a new convert of Paul. Paul had just baptized her with her entire household. As a major sponsor of the church, she persuaded Paul and his entourage to remain in her house, attending to their physical and material needs.

11. "The native people showed us unusual kindness, for they kindled a fire and welcomed us all because it had begun to rain and was cold."[54] One would have expected the native people of an island called Melita to be very hostile to Paul and his traveling companions who had escaped the shipwreck. But surprisingly, they were kind to Paul and his companions; they kindled a fire to keep them warm from the cold and possibly prepared meals for them. This attitude should be expected from the community of believers as proof of our regeneration and willingness to do our Master's will.

12. "[R]endering service with a good will as to the Lord and not to man."[55] Every act of kindness we render to others must be done in good conscience as to the Lord and not to humans. We must recognize that when we give to the poor, we are, in fact, lending to the Lord, and his good deed shall be repaid again.[56] What a promise this is! It is simply mind-blowing and fantastic! It reminds me of how the earthly ministry of Jesus was centered on giving to the poor and helping those who were disenfranchised within his neighborhood. Similarly, the Christian community must learn to be the voice of those that are voiceless and the defender of those who have no might.

53. Acts 16:15 (ESV).
54. Acts 28:2 (ESV).
55. Eph 6:7 (ESV).
56. Prov 19:17 (ESV).

13. "You shall not wrong a sojourner or oppress him, for you were sojourners in the land of Egypt."[57] Strangers who are sojourning in the land are not expected to be oppressed or maltreated even when they have become illegal because they overstayed their visa permission. The Bible wants them to be treated first as a human before any other arguments we might come up with against them.

14. "For you were called to freedom, brothers. Only do not use your freedom as an opportunity for the flesh, but through love serve one another."[58] Here the scripture reminds us of our need to be of service toward one another through good deeds. The liberty we have in Christ is not to promote fleshly desires (the mundane things of life) selfishly but look after our brethren in Christ and presumably to our significant "others."

15. "So then, as we have the opportunity, let us do good to everyone, and especially to those who are of the household of faith."[59] There are always opportunities to do good to everyone that crosses our path, although this scripture emphasizes doing good especially to the household of faith. The writer wants us to be kind to everyone regardless of their connection to our faith community. Christians must not play the blind man's game like the priest and Levite in the Parable of the Good Samaritan, who ignored the man who was robbed and left half-dead on the highway. They must particularly care for those who come to their churches for help, especially on immigration matters.

16. "He said, 'Come in, O blessed of the Lord. Why do you stand outside? For I have prepared the house and a place for the camels.'"[60] It was a common practice in ancient times to host visiting strangers who were about to take a temporary or permanent residency, as illustrated in Abraham's servant's

57. Exod 22:21; 23:9 (ESV).
58. Gal 5:13 (ESV).
59. Gal 6:10 (ESV).
60. Gen 24:31 (ESV).

narrative on a mission to seek a wife for Isaac. Rebekah and her family gladly received Abraham's servant and took good care of him and his camels while he was trying to fulfill his mission.

17. "Do not neglect to do good and to share what you have, for such sacrifices are pleasing to God."[61] There is nothing that Christians have not received from God. If they know that they have received them from God, they should be willing and freely distribute them unto others in need. Their understanding should be that they are only caretakers and faithful stewards of God's actual possessions in their care.

18. "Is it not to share your bread with the hungry and bring the homeless poor into your house; when you see the naked, to cover him, and not to hide from your flesh?"[62] The true purpose of religion is not to fast in vain but to share our meals, goods, and accommodation with the homeless poor. Lack of food and being in wants of the good things of life are sometimes what the sojourning strangers in our midst experience.

19. "The sojourner has not lodged in the street; I have opened my doors to the traveler."[63] This is undoubtedly one of the qualities that made Job the great man that he was in the East. As practicing Christians, we should endeavor to make our homes and church available for needy strangers passing by us.

20. "And you shall not strip your vineyard bare, neither shall you gather the fallen grapes of your vineyard. You shall leave them for the poor and the sojourner: I am the Lord your God."[64] One of God's greatest desires is to see Christians treat the poor, needy, and strangers in their cities and sometimes at their doorsteps with compassion and mercy. He forbade the Israelites to harvest every fruit in their vineyard during harvest time but commanded that fruits be reserved for the

61. Heb 13:16 (ESV).
62. Ias 58:7 (ESV).
63. Job 31:32 (ESV).
64. Lev 19:10 (ESV).

poor and strangers in the land. I presumed that this ought to be every citizen's disposition to the illegal alien among them.

21. "When a stranger sojourn with you in your land, you shall not do him wrong."[65] Most of the harsh policies aimed at making life unbearable for the strangers who are illegally dwelling in our land are sometimes not consistent with God's original intention. Christians should strive to be strong advocates for their brothers and sisters against unjust political leaders who failed to see the picture of God in these wandering sojourners as constituting part of human nature. Christians' love for God is most reflective of how they demonstrate love to their neighbors, specifically their wandering immigrant neighbors.

22. "You shall have the same rule for the sojourner and the native, for I am the Lord your God."[66] From God's standpoint, he wants the same rule that applies to a native-born to apply to a sojourner in the land without partiality. Biblical evidence like this scripture abounds that God is not happy at some of the ungodly policies that dehumanize the sojourning strangers in our land. Personal and collective freedom above everything else is what he wishes for all of us as a people.

23. "Now as they went on their way, Jesus entered a village. And a woman named Martha welcomed him into her house."[67] Mary and Martha, the sister of Lazarus, whom Jesus raised from the dead, were close friends of Jesus. They took a special time always to welcome Jesus into their house anytime he passed by their house. Similarly, we should be welcoming to others whom the Bible says are created in the same image of God.

24. "For truly, I say to you, whoever gives you a cup of water to drink because you belong to Christ will by no means lose his reward."[68] This scripture tells us that there is a reward attached to doing good deeds. There is no act of kindness that

65. Lev 19:33 (ESV).

66. Lev 24:22 (ESV).

67. Luke 10:38 (ESV).

68. Mark 9:41 (ESV).

goes before God unrewarded, even a kindness as small as giving a cup of water. The promise might have been given with the family of faith in mind, but we must also remember that strangers who wander into our church are potential and future households of faith. Therefore, the church should be eager to support them in the assured hope that the faithful God will reward us accordingly.

25. "And the King will answer them, Truly, I say to you, as you did it to one of the least of these my brothers, you did it to me."[69] Many people desire to serve God and do his will in their lives but are finding it hard to do. The Bible teaches that to do the will of God and serve him is to love and help our fellow humans. I am convinced that this is the greatest act of service we can ever render to God. Christians should learn how to perceive and serve God through daily encounters with their needy neighbors. God says that when Christians show these genuine acts of kindness, it is him they have demonstrated this compassion towards.

26. "She opens her hand to the poor and reaches out her hands to the needy."[70] In this scripture, we see one of the exceptional qualities possessed by the virtuous woman, according to Proverbs 31. She was always willing and ready to help a poor and needy neighbor. She was a welcoming woman who opened her doors to strangers. Christians should all strive to emulate her.

27. "That you may welcome her in the Lord in a way worthy of the saints, and help her in whatever she may need from you, for she has been a patron of many and myself as well."[71] The common expectation for the saints (believers) is to be a welcoming people not only because God commanded them to do so but also because it is part of their Christian heritage. It is supposed to be part of their cultural DNA.

69. Matt 25:40 (ESV).
70. Prov 31:20 (ESV).
71. Rom 16:2 (ESV).

28. "Gaius, who is host to the whole church and me, greets you. Erastus, the city treasurer, and our brother Quartus greet you."[72] Another strong tradition of the Christians in the Bible was that it was common for individuals with a good financial background to host many needy people within a congregation. They maintained a sense of responsibility towards those who need their financial support. Gaius belonged to the category of such people. Jairus and Cornelius in Luke 8 and Acts 10 are other examples.

Aside from the scriptures that point to my congregation's general learning about biblical hospitality, the following topics will be explored as sermon topics to contribute to their knowledge and highlight our biblical duties as responsible Christians. Some of the topics to examine are:

1. Why should Christians be hospitable?
2. What is hospitality in the church?
3. Practical ways of showing hospitality

Why Should Christians Be Hospitable?

The question of why Christians should be hospitable is very fundamental to how they carry out the act of hospitality. There are great scriptures to draw from that explicitly tell us why hospitality is a noble virtue. The practice biblically dates back to the time of Abraham and was widely practiced throughout the New Testament era among the early Christians.

There are various reasons why Christians should be hospitable. Hospitality assures believers of an earthly and eternal reward. "For truly, I say to you, whoever gives you a cup of water to drink because you belong to Christ will by no means lose his reward."[73] Second, hospitality as a sacrificial practice is such that it is always pleasing to God. Christians are not doing it to please people, but

72. Rom 16:23 (ESV).
73. Mark 9:41 (ESV).

God. "Do not neglect to do good and to share what you have, for such sacrifices are pleasing to God."[74] Finally, through its practice, people have entertained angels, which could also be "human angels." "Do not neglect to show hospitality to strangers, for thereby some have entertained angels unawares."[75] The problem with some reasons for hospitality is that they are potentially very selfish— like trying to obtain an eternal reward from God. Motive matters. Even sacrificing *everything* to the poor requiring hospitality is not enough by itself;[76] the motive behind the act is critical. So, if we are trying to obtain a reward, is it selfishness that motivates our hospitality? Or if we are trying to please God, is it a selfish desire to gain God's favor, like a sycophant? Or if we are being hospitable in the hope of entertaining angels, does our desire to interact with (or even witness to!) the supernatural have anything to do with love? Perhaps the trick is beginning to understand love as a reward in itself and the act of hospitality as a reward in itself, where any other "eternal rewards" or favors, or visitations of the supernatural, are just an additional benefit.

The unnamed rich man in the Parable of the Rich Man and Lazarus missed it at this point. He neither loved Lazarus for the sake of being in love with a neighbor nor was willing to extend hospitality to him even if it was going to be for a selfish reason. He preferred to give his dog the leftovers of his food than give to Lazarus. Hence, in the afterlife, he was not considered for eternal reward despite seeking it desperately. Because he failed to accommodate a "human angel" in the person of Lazarus, therefore, when it was a rewarding time in the afterlife, he too was excluded.[77] No doubt about it that as Africans whose worldview is deeply rooted in the afterlife, we might want to take hospitality to strangers very seriously. Thus, at least if we miss any earthly reward by chance, the otherworldly reward will be assured, which

---

74. Mark 9:41 (ESV).
75. Heb 13:2 (ESV).
76. 1 Cor 13:3 (ESV).
77. Luke 16:19–31 (ESV).

God will give to those who show kindness to their neighbors that are less privileged in the neighborhood.[78]

What Is Hospitality in the Church?

Hospitality in the church is all about welcoming the others. Christians are to demonstrate the same brotherly kindness to strangers as they would show to those of the household of faith. It is all about sharing goods with the poor, needy, prisoners, the sick, the oppressed, the marginalized, and the strangers who are sojourning within our community. Christians are to demonstrate that the act of hospitality is synonymous with the church as an agent of change. "Is it not to share your bread with the hungry and bring the homeless poor into your house; when you see the naked, to cover him, and not to hide from your flesh?"[79] As believers, we can sum up hospitality as one of the main reasons why the church exists. It is about sharing our kindness and goods with those who do not have enough to take care of their needs, particularly the wandering strangers passing by.

Practical Ways of Showing Hospitality

Hospitality is more of an act that one carries out than a state of feeling toward people. There are practical ways by which one can carry out this ancient biblical practice. Tony Merida outlined four practical ways to show Christian hospitality. They are:

1. **Welcome everyone you meet.** Merida encourages Christians to extend kind words to everyone they meet along their path and share themselves with those who need their help. Nobody should be treated as an outcast in our congregation. The religious people often accused Jesus of visiting and dining with sinners. Our religiosity should not make us insensitive but welcoming.

78. Matt 25:35–45 (ESV).
79. Isa 58:7 (ESV).

2. **Engage people.** Another practical way of showing hospitality that Merida suggests is engaging people through one-on-one connections. The idea is to invite people to come to our church and have a unique way to connect with them at their individual needs. People who come to our church are always in need of one thing or the other. The very reason they come to our church in the first place was so that their needs can be met. We have to be creative and discerning so that we can find the best possible way to engage those who come to our church door for help.

3. **Make meals a priority.** Many of Jesus' notable encounters with sinners and strangers occurred around sharing of meals.[80] Meal sharing frequently happened during his earthly ministry, like feeding the multitude through a young boy's lunch,[81] and even after his resurrection with certain disciples on the road to Emmaus.[82] In our church, we must invite people for meals/love feasts and be willing to serve them as Jesus would do. Merida suggests that meal times can often be used as a moment of connecting with our guests personally. Our church must be open and ready to utilize this avenue for ministering to strangers who visit our church.[83]

4. **Pay attention.** We meet people everywhere, every day in our lives and many of these people often go unnoticed. Therefore, we must be intentional and take some moments to slow down and connect to show kindness to those supposedly regarded as outcasts. We have to pay attention to people's clothing, diet, interests, passions, and culture with all the attendant details and particularities.[84]

---

80. Mark 2:13–17 (ESV).

81. John 6:9–14 (ESV).

82. Luke 24:13–35 (ESV).

83. Merida, "4 Practical Ways," https://www.lifeway.com/en/articles/practical-ways-to-show-christian-hospitality-tony-merida-ordinary.

84. Merida, "4 Practical Ways."

In addition to preaching sermons on hospitality, there are other specific Bible studies that I will study together with my congregation during the weekly Bible study to enhance their understanding further. The feedback that will also be generated through this Bible study will be of high significance. It will enable me to make mid-course adjustments to some of our practices that are not quite to the required standard. The Bible study topics to consider and their main ideas are presented below:

Who Is My Neighbor?

What comes to people's mind when they hear the word "neighbor"? Are we here referring to those who look very much like us and are similar to us in many ways, such as possessing the same cultural, economic, and social background or political affiliation? But what does the Bible teach about "neighbor"? In one instance, the Bible teaches us to "Love your neighbor as yourself."[85] It is useless to assume that I understand who my neighbor is, especially when viewed as people who speak, worship, and do things exactly like me. In another instance, a young lawyer questioned the status quo in Luke 10; he asked Jesus who his neighbor was. The response of Jesus is what gave birth to the Parable of the Good Samaritan, where Jesus taught that loving our neighbor is more than loving those in the same economic or social status as us, but those who are most distinct from ourselves. They are the people unwelcome by society, like the sojourning aliens within our neighborhood who do not have legal citizenship.

Our neighbor is anyone that we can help with our goods and any other form of kindness. They are the people that we do not often have any familial relationship with, but because of the kind of individual we have elected to be, choose to be there for them in their most critical time of need. "if anyone has the world's goods

85. Mark 12:31 (NIV).

and sees his brother in need, yet closes his heart against him, how does God's love abide in him."[86]

Why Is True Christian Hospitality so Important?

To ask why genuine hospitality is so important is to dig into God's fundamental first principle as the giver of every perfect gift.[87] One of the first principles of God is to give. "For God so loved the world that he gave his only Son so that whoever believes in him should not perish but have eternal life."[88] Hospitality is about giving our belongings, properties, and wealth to those most deserving in the neighborhood. It is also about receiving appreciation and a deep sense of gratitude from those that have been helped. Therefore, Christian hospitality is vital to us as believers because God first demonstrated it to all humankind. Since we are created in his image, it is just right for us to exhibit the same kind gesture that God had toward us and to our sojourning neighbors.

God hosted every human in this world as pilgrims going through a journey and decided to share the sumptuous provision of all earthly goods and treasures with all of us. Similarly, we should attend to sojourning aliens who have traveled several thousands of miles to dwell in their host country. We must be resolutely determined to ensure that they feel welcomed.

The Reward for Being Hospitable

Hospitality is one service that the African church community in the U.S. can render to strangers according to the Bible. It will not go unrewarded. "For truly, I say to you, whoever gives you a cup of water to drink because you belong to Christ will by no means lose his reward."[89] Another book of the Bible says, "do not neglect to

86. 1 John 3:17 (ESV).
87. Jas 1:17 (ESV).
88. John 3:16 (ESV).
89. Mark 9:41 (ESV).

show hospitality to strangers for by so doing some people have entertained angels unawares."[90] These are reward-oriented scriptures that push one beyond the self-serving attitude. There are apparent rewards attached to being hospitable if practiced the biblical way, even for as little effort as presenting a stranger with a cup of cold water. Providing and caring for the needs of strangers provokes divine intervention for those who practice it, and the reward could come in many shapes and forms. One such reward is the unleashing of God's big-picture plan, as in the case of Abraham when three men visited him in Genesis 18. The Bible also supports the idea that a man's gift will make room for him and bring him before great men.[91] The meaning of this is when a man uses his hospitality gift for helping a neighbor, such gift will pave a way for him in forms of many opportunities that he can tap into and make him a recognizable force within his community.

To conclude this chapter, I wish to reiterate that my overall goal is to form my congregants to adopt hospitable behavior and make hospitality a part of our DNA as we reach out to strangers for whom we intend to show care and concern until they become our neighbors. The next chapter will deal with our practical approach of carrying out this desire through our incarnational ministry outreach.

90. Heb 13:2 (ESV).
91. Prov 18:16 (ESV).

Chapter 6

The Incarnational Outreach of Justice for Jeshrun Immigration Ministry

Introduction

THIS BOOK AIMS TO design a legitimate incarnational ministry that provides resources and support to uDAIs in New England.[1] Therefore, this chapter will describe a specialized outreach program called Justice for Jeshrun Immigration Ministry (JJIM), a model patterned after the National Justice for Our Neighbors (NJ-FON), a ministry intended to serve uDAIs.

Furthermore, this chapter will discuss the transformational leadership practice of Ronald Heifetz's adaptive leadership theory to address the varied immigration cases that African immigrants bring to our attention, requiring unique solutions. Heifetz likened his adaptive leadership to the practice of medicine, which involves a diagnosis of a problem and making a suitable prescription for it. The diagnostic stage, according to Heifetz, metaphorically, requires

1. The word "legitimate" is critical to me, lest the work be undermined by shady practices or illegal behavior—the type of actions proposed by Jessica (real name redacted), the woman who approached me for help that I mentioned at the beginning. I cannot afford to be unethical or support falsehood, which to justify a shortcut is wrong.

the idea of "getting on the balcony" above the "dance floor" for a leader to get some fresh perspective about what is currently going on within one's community. Because of the varied immigration cases that will come up, it will be impossible to have one solution that fits all the cases. When different immigration cases come to our attention, each case will be dealt with on its merit by cognizance of its particularity. The goal is to encourage a mid-course adjustment where necessary, without treating every problem as a nail as though the only tool we have is a hammer.[2]

Finally, I will examine some of the future goals that I hope to pursue by utilizing the idea of Robert Quinn in his book *Deep Change: Discovering the Leader Within*. Starting an immigration ministry like JJIM will require a profound change—a kind of departure from the norms or familiar. I intend to change the way many African community churches in the U.S. have been going about addressing the immigration needs of uDAIs by deploying the deep change mantras of Quinn that he describes in his book. He argues that deep change is the type of change that is sacrificing, untiring, and demonstrable by a transformational leader who is willing to perish or die for the course he believes in. Quinn envisages that for a deep change to occur, a leader must confront the undiscussable that threatens any community's continued existence.[3] One of the national issues that seem mostly undiscussable today is the immigration issue. My church will want to be part of those who create a regular conversation around the immigration crisis confronting the nation.

What Is Incarnational Ministry?

The most straightforward definition of the Christian understanding of the word "incarnate" is that "the word became flesh and dwelt among us."[4] The Word that became flesh is Jesus, the second person

2. Heifetz, *Practice of Adaptive Leadership*, 6–8.

3. Quinn, *Deep Change*, 148–89.

4. John 1:14 (KJV). I described the nuance of this in chapter 3, under neighborhood transformation in full detail. That was the section where the

of the Trinity, who embodied the very nature of humankind and entered our world. However, for the kind of incarnational ministry that this book is propagating, the central idea is to act as Jesus would do if he were in a similar circumstance.

Jesus was physically present during his time in Palestine to demonstrate solidarity with humankind. I am convinced that this type of ministry is what his nativity in the stable symbolized—being with the lowliest of all creatures and experiencing things in their world. He not only identified with the lowliest of all people by being present with them; as later found throughout his ministry, Jesus attended to their needs as profoundly as he could when those needs arose. Here again, we are reminded of the role hospitality plays in fulfilling our mission to the underprivileged, as was the case with Jesus. The previous chapter dwelt on the theology of hospitality. This section elaborates on the practical aspect of hospitality as it pertains to the undocumented African community in New England. "This is the kind of life you have been invited into, the kind of life Christ lived. He suffered everything that came his way so you would know that it could be done, and also know how to do it, step-by-step."[5]

In Pursuit of an Immigration Outreach

I will develop an outreach program specifically for African immigrants, whose voices have been mostly unheard and have been the object of systemic targeting by unfavorable policies from the USCIS, through a deliberate act of discrimination from access to food, healthcare, and housing.[6]

The immigration challenges of Africans have become a vital ministry that requires active participation by me. At the local level, my church, not deterred by its current size, will work to reach out to various broader community segments. Our sincere hope is that

idea of God-with-us—"Immanuel"—was discussed. I will refrain from repeating it here in this section.

5. 1 Pet 2:21 (MSG).

6. Francois, "Green Cards Only."

all the different arms of our outreach and ministries will become very active within the next ten years. I am convinced that tackling the lingering crisis that African immigrants face in the U.S. today is a worthy ministry for me to pursue. I honestly believe that getting involved in this ministry will allow me to make my mark in the transformation of people's lives, specifically among African communities. A robust theological understanding of the need to stand up for strangers and those on the marginal side of life is strong now and serves as an energizing motivator for me.

However, the greatest challenge that I have had to face is a common assumption that immigrants who have become undocumented and illegal aliens are always to blame for their predicament. Society tend to forget that these are people who left their home countries because of economic hardship, political unrest beyond their own making, and direct credible threats to their physical safety, but are now vigorously seeking greener pastures elsewhere, just to get by. Such was the case of an earlier cited case of a uDAI named Jessica, who brought a proposal to me to write an affidavit on her behalf and that of her "arranged husband" that was not real. Although I understand her plight and the hardship she might be going through, I also believe that there should be a possible exception for them to negotiate an alternative path to citizenship, as Firth argued.[7] Honestly, I felt that her proposal was very contradictory to my convictions of what transformational practices need to be, and of the sanctity of marriage.

But I was in that moment of contradiction face-to-face with Joseph Fletcher's notion of an ethic of intuition rooted in love. Fletcher has inferred that love decides "then and there" what is the most loving thing to do under such a specific situation. This approach, according to Fletcher, does not necessarily draw from a rich theological context other than the pure connection to Christian love.[8] The most loving thing to do seemed to be to decline that approach for resolving her immigration challenge.

7. Firth, *Including the Stranger*, 22.
8. Wogaman, *Christian Ethics*, 235.

Similarly, Paul Lehmann, whose work could be said to be a step further to Fletcher's proposition, foresaw ethics in a "Christian context," which connotes the situation confronted on the one hand and the theological context on the other. He argues that when the two conflict with one another, then Christians are obligated to do what God would do at that moment in time.[9] As I pondered on the proposal brought before me by this beloved African immigrant, I reflected on the motto of Rev. Henry Maxwell, the fictional character in Charles Sheldon's book *In His Steps*: "'What would Jesus do?' Our aim will be to act just as He would if He was in our places, regardless of immediate results."[10] Of course, it became apparent to me that I would not accept such a proposal because I reasoned that Jesus would not support falsehood to justify wrong behavior. The obvious thing going forward is the sad news that not every potential immigration case would be supported by me as I would have loved judging by Jessica's experience.

The Incarnational Ministry Set Up

As an expression of that biblical Christian impulse to be hospitable, our church shall set up a Justice for Jeshrun Immigration Ministry (JJIM).[11] The immigration ministry setup will take National Justice for Our Neighbors (NJFON) as a model. NJFON is a ministry arm under the United Methodist Church.[12] To achieve my aim of setting up this ministry, I arranged a Zoom meeting with one of the leaders of the NJFON clinic located in the United Methodist Church Belmont-Watertown, Massachusetts, to gain firsthand experience

9. Wogaman, *Christian Ethics*, 230.

10. Sheldon, *In His Steps*, 22–24.

11. The acronym JJIM reflect the migratory journey of Jeshurun which is the name given to Jacob and his descendants, similar to many immigrants' experience today.

12. See https://njfon.org. This is the national website for the National Justice for Our Neighbors, a ministry arm under the United Methodist Church with fifty clinics across seventeen sites in twelve states and Washington, DC, and over sixty staff members mostly lawyers, handling over ten thousand cases, with hundreds of volunteers from local congregations and communities.

of how the ministry is coordinated. Rev. Gary Richards explained how the church he currently serves at, UMC Belmont-Watertown, has had a long history of immigrants and refugee ministry. He was fortunate to have worked previously in immigration ministry with the former pastor of his congregation, who helped start New England Justice for Our Neighbors—We Chang (now a district superintendent for Boston area). They worked together for several years to organize the New England JFON.[13]

The New England JFON is one site out of approximately eighteen locations throughout the country. NJFON serves as an umbrella organization, and they are associated with the NJFON by using Justice for Our Neighbors' name. The New England site does receive technical and financial support, but it is a small portion compared to their actual budget. NJFON is a United Methodist Church Immigration Ministry funded at the national level by the United Methodist Committee on Relief (UMCOR), a long-standing denominational organization that has served immigrants and refugees for decades. Over twenty years ago, they decided to incorporate legal services for immigrants in dire need, giving free quality legal services. The way they are organized involves a typical local church serving as the actual clinic site. The local church is the one that will provide the primary ministry, which is hospitality such as the opening of doors, arranging a comfortable private space for the attorney, creating a comfortable waiting area for visitors, food, and childcare—in general fostering a safe and comfortable space. The organization hires attorneys. It has to raise significant money even though the attorneys are not paid the going rate. They do have to be compensated and provided with benefits. Normally, a substantial part of the ministry would involve raising funds for these attorneys.

However, the New England JFON uses a different model. They do not hire their attorneys, because Massachusetts has a very robust legal services community. Every urban area has a legal services program, which is great news for us at the JJIM. The Massachusetts government and the private bar have been very

13. Gary Richards, interview by author, June 24, 2021.

generous over the years to fund these legal service programs. They are by and large those dealing with civil legal issues that poor communities often struggle with. These include eviction, public assistance, cash assistance, disability benefits, education, health, mental health, domestic violence, and other issues that people wrestle with that require a good attorney. Because of the availability of these resources, the New England JFON felt it would not be necessary to hire their attorneys but instead contract with experts that are already in the neighborhood. The attorneys are already working for one or two organizations and are also working for the New England JFON. Their church-based clinics pre-COVID were opened in Springfield in the western part of the state, Worcester in the central region, in the North Shore areas Lawrence and Lowell, finally in Metro Boston, Woburn. Before the COVID outbreak, they were at the final stage of conversation with Providence, Rhode Island, with Open Table UMC. The general idea is for them to continue to increase the capacity of local legal services programs to provide legal services to those who are most qualified.

The purpose is to afford the newcomers—the immigrant migrants and asylum seekers—other types of free quality legal services whenever the need arises, whether about eviction, healthcare, or domestic violence requiring legal action. There is a whole staff of attorneys, not just immigration attorneys, at each legal service. Because they use the local churches for their operations, i.e., for clinic sites, New England JFON also organizes volunteers that are around on each site before an attorney will appear, ensuring the clinics run very smoothly. For instance, when the clinic is open and the attorney is in their office, the volunteers will welcome and prepare the initial intake paperwork for the visitor and the person scheduled to see the attorney. The visitor is ushered to the private space to be seen by the attorney; every single visitor gets advice and counsel for free. They can spend one hour or a little more than an hour with an experienced immigration attorney. After that, the immigration attorney will tell the individual if there is a legal remedy or not. Sometimes the case is not one that these attorneys can handle because of complexities or limited resources. The volunteer attorney may recommend another attorney to be contacted or give the visitor a list of pro bono attorneys if it is a case that an experienced attorney can still handle with more effort.

Usually, it is not every case that the attorney sees through the JFON clinics, but JFON representatives can pursue a long-term legal representation. In an asylum case, a case of domestic violence, or an unaccompanied juvenile crossing the border, such cases are worked up and prepared back in the law office of these non-profit organizations. The church only serves as the entryway to the legal services. Of course, this type of arrangement frees the church from having to worry about files, cabinets, and all the necessary storage space for confidential legal documents.

Because the New England JFON has uDAIs as the largest group patronizing their immigration clinics, JJIM has begun a liaison with them, working together as partners in processing some of the uDAIs' immigration issues. The type of strategy emphasized here is essential because the uDAIs are the largest group patronizing their immigration clinics.[14] The clinic strategy is good because it allows for the dissemination of helpful information for people for free, and this ultimately prevents them from spending money on issues that are not necessary.

The ministry model presented in this book was most efficient during the pre-COVID era. The aftermath of COVID affected how the clinic had to be run. The advent of the COVID immediately led to the abrupt stoppage of operation of the clinics during the pandemic. New England JFON quickly seized the opportunity of the pandemic to address the backlog of cases that have been pending resolution. This may be good news for some undocumented immigrants, but not so good for the new entrants as new cases were no longer accepted because of the growing risk of keeping people on the clinic site during the pandemic. I am of the opinion that immigration ministry should not be in this kind of situation particularly during this time (pandemic) that uDAIs users need help and a place where they can find support. A proactive measure has

14. Gary Richards, interview by Olusegun Osineye.

to be developed that will resolve all health-related safety concerns while smooth immigration ministry can still be ongoing.

In summary, through JJIM's core mission, my congregation shall provide a safe space for immigrants in our neighborhood, taking our cue from the way New England JFON is set up. Our church shall welcome strangers with open arms and be a place where the hope of those seeking a better life can be reignited by providing free or low-cost immigration services, especially to vulnerable African immigrants.

My church shall recommend uDAIs who come through our door to our liaison partners at New England JFON as they may require being seen by lawyers. Similarly, through our food pantry outreach, we shall have volunteers and donations (especially non-perishable food items and toiletries such as toothpaste, shampoo, and diapers). Once people come to take part in a free meal, they can also see a lawyer or make an appointment to see the lawyer. We shall have the same type of model with a health clinic, with a doctor to give medical advice and possible prescriptions to those African immigrants who patronize our clinic for free health care.

Because many undocumented people fear the idea of being identified publicly by seeing a lawyer, JJIM will adopt the Zoom meeting room option to establish trust with clients. Furthermore, the church space and friendly atmosphere will also provide spiritual succor to those undocumented immigrants in deep spiritual deprivation. Our goal is not to impose our religious beliefs on individuals who come for help, but we will offer spiritual care and comfort to those who seek such through our weekly Sunday worship service, weekly Bible study and prayer meetings, and of course special individualized spiritual and trauma management counseling sessions.

JJIM shall operate under the guidance of a board of directors with limited full-time professional workers and consulting compassionate attorneys who will be engaged on a part-time basis in New England. Fortunately for us, JJIM will not need to hire a full-time attorney because Massachusetts has a robust legal services community. Since the immigration ministry is much more than providing legal services, we will focus on affordable shelter and less expensive rental options. If this is impossible, JJIM will provide information on how and where immigrants can get such information.

One area where we will need to spend time and the bulk of our energy is fundraising. To this end, our primary source of funding shall be offerings and donations from church members and their families and friends. We shall identify different organizations that can make donations regularly for us, which we can continue to build upon over time and have them as part of our donor base. JJIM's board of directors shall also assist in organizing around fundraising through dinners or other such meaningful programs. During one of our specialized Soul-Lifting/Musical Annual Fiestas, to be called Nativity Fiesta Night in December, sales of tickets will be open for all and sundry to participate. The program will incorporate story-telling that will feature foreign- and U.S.-born residents sharing immigrant experiences. It will offer spiritual support through inspirational music and dancing. There will be feasting and merry-making because we believe that celebration is an essential part of the ministry of hospitality. Then, of course, there shall be donations and financial pledges from supporters of the church.

JJIM will begin with three ways to minister to the immigrants in New England. First, it will allow an immigration attorney to meet with individuals or families once every three months either on the church property or through Zoom; both strategies will be deployed, especially since the advent of COVID-19. Anyone who has questions will be able to schedule an appointment by phone or through email. The clinic shall demonstrate hospitality by offering a meal and activities for children who accompany their parents.

Second, JJIM will launch a series of educational events called the "monthly breakfast fellowship" to address particular concerns within the undocumented immigrant community. These will include seminars and workshops by immigration experts on how immigrants can transition to becoming legal residents. Topics like "know your rights," "humanitarian immigration remedies available in the U.S.," and others will be addressed. Equally important is information about what medical services are available for immigrants, whether a person is a legal resident or not. Another issue entails how to enroll children in public schools without fear of reprisal, navigating how to find affordable housing, etc. Topics will be decided by those who attend the forums. The frequency of these educational events shall be monthly, during the last Saturday of every month.

Third, JJIM will work intensively with the local church. It will help the congregation become aware of the need to be present and available to our neighbors. One thing that is valuable to a newcomer is friendship. Our undocumented immigrant friends need someone they can call upon when they are lonely. Also, when they have a particular need or when they need to go to someplace but are not sure about the possible outcome, or maybe they are looking for a license or job or going to school for the first time.

The plan is to have an open door, especially with those trained to have an immigrant experience to walk alongside, not in front of them or pushing from the back. The church should go alongside our undocumented immigrant friends when they step into new and unfamiliar territory to develop a relationship. JJIM will seek to energize the congregants to get involved with all the complexities of being with our undocumented immigrant community.

JJIM, through the church, will aim to provide an accompaniment network that can support and accompany people as they deal with immigration hearings, Immigration and Customs Enforcement (ICE) check-ins, court cases, and other stressful situations. Not only can congregants donate such items as food, clothing, and toiletries, but part of the church's income shall be for those who come to the church for immigration assistance or extra help. The local church can also organize prayer vigils at the ICE detention center to show support and solidarity with those detained by ICE and reaffirm our commitment to the pursuit of justice on behalf of the arrested.

Additionally, church members can also help staff our events. JJIM's close interface with the local church is desirable because the intention is to create the awareness that the ministry arm is not solely an independent body severed from the church but part and parcel of it.

JJIM shall seek to implement its threefold mission by abiding by and showing our true fidelity to the following principles: excellent policies, ethical practices, advocacy, collaborative initiative, consulting, and accountability throughout our church network in New England. For instance, doing immigration ministry can easily slide into the practices of some unethical behavior, such as the one I previously mentioned in this book. Therefore, in JJIM, these principles will advance our mission in the three concrete ministries of providing lawyers for vulnerable immigrants, organizing workshops that could provide timely intervention in specific immigration challenges, and a food/clothing pantry. The JJIM general strategic plan is summarized under these headings:

1. **Excellent Policies:** Our policies at JJIM will be offered in such a manner that they will give priority to undocumented immigrants from Africa. It has been observed that immigrants from South and Central America, as well as Asia and the Caribbean, have been catered for through outreach provided by National Justice for Our Neighbors (NJFON, a United Methodist Immigration Ministry) and through Church World Service (CWS). Although Africans also benefit from their services, it is not widely publicized among Africans. It is essential, therefore, to design our policies to meet the needs of African immigrants by African service providers like JJIM.

2. **Ethical Practices:** "Best practices" shall be our watchword at JJIM. We shall always endeavor to go through the most ethical routes to bring justice and equality to vulnerable undocumented African immigrants.

3. **Advocacy:** We acknowledge that we are in a disadvantaged position to change governmental policies against undocumented immigrants because we are currently unorganized as people. Our effort will be to begin raising awareness at our local level to create a formidable platform to enhance the rights and dignity of all individuals. Because of the enormity

of the cost involved and the complexities of individual immigration cases, an all-encompassing strategic plan will require a unique structural approach to tackle African immigrants' problems. In that design, Robert Quinn's notion of effecting a profound change will be a significant consideration, where he challenges people to confront the undiscussable, which—unless addressed—cause situations to stagnate and slow down.[15] In this context, immigration discourse on a national scale has many competing sentiments, which has made it mostly undiscussable. Because of the rhetoric of resentment of "others" who are not like "us," we are determined to go all the way to initiate these undiscussable issues that are already threatening our common humanity and peaceful coexistence. By lending our unique voice and perspective on the importance of helping strangers, and upholding the dignity of our humanity, we hope that favorable dispositions toward immigrants will begin to be cultivated by the ruling class and the general populace at large.

4. **Collaborative Initiatives:** We shall endeavor to collaborate with our church network across New England for a broader scope of impact. We shall facilitate partnership with a reputable law firm that is very successful in handling immigration cases, the American Immigration Lawyers Association. We will also seek partnerships with other groups and individuals that can provide volunteer services or prospective donors.

5. **Consulting:** We will open a consulting clinic at our church venue where vulnerable African immigrants can come and fill out a form, which will be made optional to provide identity protection for them as much as possible. The ultimate goal will be to connect them to the right resources to help handle their specific immiration issues.

6. **Accountability:** We will hope to be accountable first to God, to our church family, the African community in the U.S., and the larger society for the promotion of justice, equity, and

15. Quinn, *Deep Change*, 176–89.

progress. Any form of recklessness will not be entertained or allowed to thrive in the way JJIM will carry out its incarnational immigration outreach among uDAIs in New England.

Ronald Heifetz's Adaptive Leadership Practice

Immigration cases vary in reality. There are hardly two identical immigration cases because a case can present itself as a complex human migratory experience. To this end, I will adopt the transformational leadership practice of Ronald Heifetz's adaptive leadership to address the varied immigration cases that require a unique and specified solution. As I reflect on the plight of Johnson, the character in my case study, and many other immigrants of African descent, one of the central leadership theories and practices that comes to mind is the practice of adaptive leadership, proposed principally by Ronald Heifetz.

The main argument of Heifetz is that when a leader steps aside for a moment to observe a current problem from an outsider's perspective, doing so will allow the leader to make a mid-course adjustment to the happenings within the community rather than wait until there is a major crisis.[16]Heifetz's leadership theory applies to the situation of Johnson. Johnson (real name redacted) is a young college graduate from Nigeria who was on the verge of losing his F-1 visa status because he lacked the opportunity to find a place to work. Johnson was qualified to work for three years in the U.S. as a STEM student for Optional Practical Training (OPT), but his attempt to find a suitable job ended in disappointment on two occasions.

Despite our grand vision to support immigrants of African descent, my church met failure in his case. I like to think of it now not as a failure but as a learning process. Heifetz likes to think of it as an experiment or, as it is often depicted in the twenty-first-century business management notion, "design thinking." Design thinking is a concept whereby a failed experiment

16. Heifetz, *Practice of Adaptive Leadership*, 6–8.

is not considered as a failure, but a learning process, which will ultimately enable an organization to come up with ideal solutions to the current challenges. In my church context, several of such failed experiments will ultimately yield possible solutions that will eventually solve the current immigration challenges that often confront immigrants from Africa.[17] There is less advocacy for immigrants from Africa than for their counterparts from Asia, South America, or Central America. The lack of advocacy has ensured that the voices of immigrants from Africa are not heard and has heightened their vulnerability against stringent measures from the major proponents of anti-immigrant laws.

The diocese under whose umbrella my church operates is partly to be blamed for the unavailability of ministry that fights the plight of immigrants, particularly those of African descent. Most of the members in our diocese are immigrants, and yet to date no substantial ministry advocates for these vulnerable groups. Perhaps our diocese could make a concerted effort together to address these people, who so closely resemble Jesus Christ the immigrant in their present predicament, as in the case of Johnson, for example. Jesus was an alien seeking asylum, just like many of these African immigrants. And when my diocese fails to advocate for any meaningful opportunity for ministry in this area, we are failing Christ himself. "I was a stranger, and you did not welcome me."[18] My diocese is busy focusing on individual salvation but is neglecting social advocacy, such as providing an expensive ministry that helps the homeless or illegal immigrants. But my church family wants to be an exception. We have decided to take a different path by wholeheartedly embracing these ministries.

My pastoral support for Johnson failed principally because of a lack of financial resources and partly due to the absence of active and vibrant volunteers who could help enrich that aspect of the ministry. I am aware that financial resources play a crucial role because it is almost impossible to provide a ministry without money. Money is that essential tool that will move our church plans from

---

17. Heifetz, *Practice of Adaptive Leadership*, 28–37.
18. Matt 25:43 (ESV).

paper to a flourishing mission. For instance, ministry to homeless immigrants requires sufficient money to provide such things as food, shelter, clothes, and toiletries. Lack of money could place a barrier to these potential ministries.

Again, providing immigrants with competent and compassionate attorneys can be very difficult. Similarly, discerning the right resources on a case-by-case basis may be very hard to do. Engaging with the possibilities of these social services at present in my church is very challenging and this perhaps accounted for our failure in meeting Johnson's need. This is not to say that I lack the required support to carry on with the ministry. My church leadership team has been very supportive of the idea. Every time we have an immigration outreach workshop, they are usually present to participate in the program and provide volunteer services where necessary. Rev. Gary Richards, as one of the leaders of the New England JFON, has been offering collaborative support to JJIM when needed. Despite the prevailing challenges, we are more than determined to take up the different scenarios that the ministry present through adaptive leadership and hope to count on our achievements within the next decade.

Establishing a Deep Change

I would like to conclude this chapter by proposing some of the future goals that I wish to pursue by recalling the idea of Robert Quinn in his book *Deep Change: Discovering the Leader Within*, where he argues that deep change is the type of change that is sacrificing, untiring, and verifiable by a transformational leader who is willing to perish or die for the course that he believes in.[19] I am deeply concerned about the potential ministries that exist to help African immigrants in this country. I am specifically glad because the ministry has scriptural ground on which to pursue its execution—the flight of Jesus and his parents to Egypt.[20]

19. Quinn, *Deep Change*, 148.
20. Matt 2:13–15 (KJV).

Quinn, similarly, postulates four primary and competing roles of a leader, which I hope to adopt, principles that will determine the direction and future of our community. The roles are vision casting, motivating, analyzing, and task managing.[21] I will engage in ongoing vision casting with the leadership team of our church about how we want the ministry to the immigrants to emerge in my setting. The plan will involve serious motivation for all our paid staff and volunteer workers. As Heifetz suggests, I will take occasional moments to step on the balcony to uncover what is going on in this area of ministry to make mid-course adjustments when necessary. Finally, I will be proactive rather than reactive to manage our resources efficiently so that our tasks are carried out as efficiently as possible.

Quinn also envisaged that for a deep change to occur, the leader must learn how to confront the undiscussable that threatens any community's continued existence. He asserts that the undiscussable are typical problems that cause a community to stagnate and slow down.[22] The immigration discourse is one major social discourse that the U.S. government is most perplexed with at the moment. There is obvious resentment on all sides in the U.S. today. Our church wants to be among those to initiate these undiscussable issues that threaten our common and peaceful coexistence. Our church family wants to be regarded as one socially responsible mission, hence our desire to pursue this ministry.

Evaluation of Results

A year after implementing the JJIM programs, I will evaluate them in some specific and tangible ways, such as analyzing spiritual growth in the congregation. I hope to document increased relationships between church members and needy immigrants and access to supportive resources by undocumented immigrants. The parish church council members, the JJIM leaders, volunteer members

---

21. Quinn, *Deep Change*, 148.
22. Quinn, *Deep Change*, 176–89.

from the congregation, and some selected immigrants will be called together to have a roundtable conversation around the three areas we identify to see visible progress and improvement.

First, I will seek to know how deeply entrenched is the congregation's biblical hospitality practice, especially how much and how far my congregation has adopted the spiritual stance of hospitality since the inception of the JJIM. Second, I will anecdotally evaluate the increase and the degree of relationship between my congregation and undocumented immigrants. I will measure our resulting successes through testimonies of privately initiated help and support from my congregants to undocumented immigrants. I want to see a hospitality culture reflected by entrenched hospitality practices in the congregation. Furthermore, I hope to see mutual spiritual growth as a byproduct of our hospitality tradition both within my congregation and toward undocumented immigrants.

Finally, I will evaluate our effectiveness by surveying the African immigrant community's ability to access food, cheap housing, immigration counsel, affordable healthcare, and good public schools for their children through the platform of JJIM efficiently. How much uDAIs are able to utilize our wide range of activities will be a good yardstick to measure how we are doing. It is hoped that with this strategy in place we will be able to possibly identify where improvement will be required for future optimum performance.

Conclusion

This chapter has aimed to challenge my congregation to strive to do more and possibly be a role model for other African church communities to go and do likewise by becoming more present to the needs of our immigrant brothers and sisters in the neighborhood. The ultimate goal for us as a church through JJIM is to provide for uDAIs' physical, emotional, and spiritual needs. The African church communities are not there yet! Most African churches do not even understand the necessity of an immigration ministry. They are satisfied with getting people saved, while such people's social status is in great jeopardy. We have to begin from somewhere, and creating this awareness and intentionally participating in the incarnational ministry is an excellent place to start. There are many inherent benefits that my church stands to gain if we pursue immigration needs in the African community as our core ministry. One of such benefits is a thriving African community. As we count our gains and other benefits, the greatest obstacles standing in our way are the various government policies that target the vulnerabilities of immigrants, policies that stifle access to self-sufficiency, a livable wage, healthcare, and housing to mention only a few.

Conclusion

What Is the Vocation of African Immigrants?

As I HAVE ARGUED throughout this book, the church is not the place where we carry out some good and noble activities for religiosity's sake. The church should be set up to live out purposefully the true meaning of her creed—to feed the hungry, clothe the naked, shelter the homeless, visit the sick, and help strangers.[1] In my context, we are already involved in these biblical deeds. Still, there is a greater mission that I want to develop with the African immigrant community that entails more than feeding the hungry and clothing the naked based on the injunctions of Jesus Christ in Matthew 25:35–40. The grander idea is how African immigrants who have fled oppressive rule and economic hardship in Africa can give back to their home country. As I conceive it, the bigger picture is for African immigrants, who have been helped to gain financial stability in their country of residence through supportive efforts from the churches, to begin thinking of initiating the social transformation of African society. The process of building the broken walls and the ruined cities of Africa is even now an immutable priority, and

---

1. Matt 25:35–40 (KJV).

128

building this project for African diasporas and expatriates is the first part of such a larger mission.

The effort that has gone into writing this book is a clarion call to my congregation and the African church communities in the U.S. of what we should be doing as a community together. As I acknowledged earlier, my church, since its inception, has distinguished itself as a mission agency established to cater for African immigrants' needs in our neighborhood. But the more I began to study people's global movement, the more I see now that a dramatic shift is possible in our responsibility as a church. I have realized that my church should not just be meeting the needs of African immigrants. Still, a platform for immigrants whom our church has helped could also provide the foundation for an agenda to give back to their homeland friends and families in Africa. There is a note of caution here: since Africa is a very diverse society, I do not expect diaspora immigrants to think of giving back in a continental-wide adventure. I want to presume that the diaspora will operate in an isolated manner, focusing on their immediate cultural group for social development rather than on the continent as a whole. It must also be noted that while giving back maybe a natural focus for first-generation immigrants, it might not be an acceptable practice among second-generation immigrants, who often see themselves as bona fide citizens of their country of birth rather than the country of their parents' origin.

I must admit that this new understanding is outside this book's scope. I do not want to digress into all those details. It may eventually become a new research area for interested researchers to investigate further. However, my immediate strategic plan will be to create awareness and organize my congregation toward extending the same kindness from the Africans in New England to African communities in the neighborhood of their homelands. The idea is to remind them to remember their origins and develop social plans to help their homeland after attaining financial independence and stability.

Although my primary audience is my congregation, I still intend to make this exercise a community-wide endeavor for those Africans in the diaspora, using my congregation as the starting point. The resistance that I anticipate is the pessimism of many African immigrants, including members of my congregation—pessimism about implementing effective social programs that can directly impact people's lives in Africa. A critical part of the pessimism is grounded in bad governance and bureaucratic bottlenecks in many African societies.

Theological assumptions that I brought into this have been shaped by Andrew Walls's two opposing views of migration, Adamic and Abrahamic migration, in his book *Crossing Cultural Frontiers: Studies in the History of World Christianity*. Adamic migration, according to Walls, is marked by a forceful displacement and involuntary migration that leads to loss of home, loss of well-being, and loss of expectation.[2]

In contrast, Abrahamic migration signifies hope for a better future and anticipation of a good life.[3] The theological grounding of Andrew Walls perfectly depicts the state of many African immigrants today. Some have been displaced due to wars, religious persecution, oppressive governments, economic deprivation, dislocation, etc. In contrast, others have moved because of the promise of a bright future that is on the way—like students who want to attend top foreign universities to seek employment where their area of specialty is recognized and needed, such as medical doctors, nurses, and engineers. But as I read about Abrahamic migration, my mind was flooded with various questions and ideas. I started thinking, was Abrahamic migration really about the expectation of a good life? Suddenly I saw a big hole as I continued to ponder! I began to see a "brain drain" problem in Abraham's native home in Ur, Mesopotamia. Immediately I began to contextualize it to the brain drain that some nations of the world are experiencing today because their governments, like India, Pakistan, and Nigeria, have not yet tapped their vast potential. So, when I began to ponder Andrew Walls's theological depiction of the Adamic and Abrahamic migration experience, the reality

2. Walls, "Theology of Migration?," 40.
3. Walls, "Theology of Migration?," 41.

dawned on me. I asked, was Abrahamic migration only an expectation of a good life? Or are we seeing another form of brain drain of great minds from Nigeria, Ghana, Ethiopia, and other nations of the world that are yet to harness their vast untapped human potentials? While Abrahamic migration was a gain for him and his succeeding generations, how might we begin to quantify the loss that it brought to his native home in Ur of Mesopotamia? A giveback movement stands with the prophecy of the prophet Isaiah in the book of Isaiah 61:1–7, where the dispersed Jews would one day build the old ruined places of Israel and restore the formerly desolate places. Nehemiah and Ezra come to mind in connection to the realization of this prophecy. Both of them were instrumental in mobilizing the diaspora Jews in their times to rebuild the broken walls and the house of God in Jerusalem. Nehemiah and Ezra failed to acknowledge each other and seem to have worked independently of one another, even though the biblical dating of their activities puts them in Jerusalem at the same time.[4]

Nehemiah, the Builder of Jerusalem Broken Walls

When the news of Jerusalem's broken walls reached Nehemiah from the Jews who had fled from the anguish that came upon the city (Jerusalem) in Shushan, Nehemiah broke down in tears and mourned for several days, seeking the face of God on how best to approach the situation in their homeland. After getting clarity of direction of what needed to be done, he summoned all the Jews in the diaspora together, particularly those residing in Shushan. With the permission of King Artaxerxesin, whose presence he constantly presented himself to, he provided the required leadership for the take-off of the project among the dispersed Jews. He charged them to come together so that they could build the walls of Jerusalem that were broken so they would no longer be a reproach among other nations. The people agreed with him as they

---

4. Bandstra, *Reading the Old Testament*, 466.

rose to commence the rebuilding process.[5] What Nehemiah and the Jews in the diaspora did is similar to what I am envisioning for the Africans in New England to do in the various localities of their homeland. I want them to bring transformation to their local communities by rebuilding the ruined places.

Ezra and the Return of the Exile

The plan to rebuild the house of God in Jerusalem unexpectedly came from Cyrus, the king of Persia, who believed that God had given him oversight over all the kingdoms of the earth. He was convinced that God had charged him to rebuild the Jerusalem temple, which had been destroyed by his predecessor, Nebuchadnezzar. He became the rallying point for all the dispersed Jews, encouraging them to pull their resources together for the sake of rebuilding the house of God in Jerusalem. King Cyrus personally led the way by supporting the rebuilding process by offering the resources that his predecessor, Nebuchadnezzar, had stolen from the house of God previously in Jerusalem for the project.[6]

On the other hand, the exiles in Persia returned to Jerusalem to rebuild the temple under this new dispensation. Undoubtedly, Yahweh's blessings on them were full and overflowing such that he did not allow them to return empty-handed. He enabled them to pull their resources together for the task ahead. There is a great lesson to be learned here by the U.S. government, who, like Cyrus, often perceive themselves as having oversight over all the nations of the world and the Africans residing in the U.S. They must both work hand in hand to initiate a rebuilding process in Africa. The idea of rebuilding may not necessarily be a continental-wide agenda but may be undertaken at the different local levels by diaspora Africans.

5. Neh 1:2–4, 17–18 (KJV).
6. Ezra 1:2–8 (KJV).

Contemporary Jewish Communities in the Diaspora

The good deeds of the contemporary Jewish communities of the Jewish diaspora, especially in the U.S., have had a profound impact on my understanding of what should be the vocation of African immigrants. In his book *The Jewish Phenomenon: 7 Keys to Enduring Wealth of a People*, Steven Silbiger writes that "to safeguard and enhance the health of their community, Jews zealously deploy their wealth and their time for both charity and social action."[7] He argues that generosity acts among the Jews are highly commendable, considering their population's small size. Unfortunately, conventional prejudice sees Jews as close-fisted, but in reality they are the most philanthropic ethnic group in America.[8] Silbiger credits the ability of Jews to organize and utilize economic power as one of the significant sources of strong Jewish-American community ties today. He opines that "the support of Israel is of paramount importance to Jews and receives very generous support."[9] Again, he writes that "when Jews around the world are threatened, Jewish-Americans quickly send money, as was the case with Ethiopian Jews facing starvation and the Russian Jews' resettlement needs after the fall of the Soviet Union."[10] Silbiger also states that "Jews are taught that charity is an obligation rooted in social justice, not in love or pity for their fellow man."[11] Charity is obligated to advocate for social justice by the Jews because of their long history of suffering discrimination.[12]

The African community in the U.S. has a great deal to learn from its Jewish counterparts on giving back to their home countries and supporting communities anywhere in this world. Churches should not be obsessed with elephant projects such as building big auditoriums, building expensive houses for their

7. Silbiger, *Jewish Phenomenon*, 35.
8. Silbiger, *Jewish Phenomenon*, 35.
9. Silbiger, *Jewish Phenomenon*, 35.
10. Silbiger, *Jewish Phenomenon*, 37.
11. Silbiger, *Jewish Phenomenon*, 37.
12. Silbiger, *Jewish Phenomenon*, 38.

pastors, and buying private jets and exotic cars for pastors. As my ideal for the African community in the diaspora, I am proposing that African churches provide help through acts of generosity for African immigrants who have fled oppressive rule and economic marginalization by the ruling classes in Africa. In return, when those immigrants gain financial independence and stability, the church should tutor them on the importance of giving back to the homeland in Africa through good deeds, just like diaspora Jews. African communities can engage in social actions that improve people's quality of life through good educational support by financing privately funded schools, healthcare facilities, small-scale businesses that can provide jobs, etc. Doing these will, in part, fulfill the divine mandate of the church here on earth.

I had always thought that God would guide me to devote my ministry to helping African immigrants. But living the theological proposition of Abrahamic migration by Andrew Walls also empowers African immigrants to give back to their homeland in Africa after gaining financial independence and stability in their country of residence. I am convinced that Africans can only restore the African continent's deplorable state when the dispersed diaspora plays a significant part by transforming the native people's lives and, in doing so, finding personal transformation for themselves. We have seen this in history. Jews in the diaspora were the ones who mobilized themselves and pulled their resources together to form a new nation of Israel in 1948 after years of persecution and ethnic cleansing by the Nazis led by Adolf Hitler. I have discovered that my community (African community in the U.S.) lacks the impetus to go all the way to effect the needed change that is desirable in Africa, despite the enormous financial and human resources at their disposal. We do not lack in talents and resources to make these changes. What we need is proper coordination of these vast resources, and I am willing to be part of those who will coordinate this movement of giving back.

Bibliography

"Africa/United States: African Immigrant Population on Rise in US." *Asia News Monitor*, February 22, 2017.

Anderson, Mary. "Hospitality Theology." *The Christian Century* 115:19 (July 1, 1998) 643.

Arthur, John A. *Invisible Sojourners: African Immigrant Diaspora in the United States*. Westport, CT: Praeger, 2000.

Bandstra, Barry L. *Reading the Old Testament*. 4th ed. Belmont, CA: Wadsworth Cengage, 2009.

Bergquist, Linda, and Allan Karr. *Church Turned Inside Out: A Guide for Designers, Refiners, and Re-Aligners*. San Francisco: Wiley, 2010.

Boak, Josh. "Biden Calls for Bipartisan Action on Pathway to Citizenship." *U.S News & World Report*, July 2, 2021, https://www.usnews.com/news/politics/articles/2021-07-02/biden-to-host-naturalization.

Brown, Tim, and Barry Katz. "Change by Design." *The Journal of Product Innovation* 28:3 (2011) 381–83.

Budiman, Abby. "Key Findings about U.S. Immigrants." Pew Research Center, 2020.

Burnett, John. "U.S. Churches Offer Safe Haven for a New Generation of Immigrants." NPR, February 9, 2016. https://www.npr.org/2016/02/09/466145280/u-s-churches-offer-safe-haven-for-a-new-generation-of-migrants.

Carroll, R., et al. *Immigrant Neighbors among Us: Immigration across Theological Traditions*. Eugene, OR: Wipf & Stock, 2015.

Central Intelligence Agency. *The World Factbook*. Washington, DC: CIA, 2018.

Chavez, Marta S. "Latin American Migration." *Apuntes Reflexiones Teologicas Des de El Margen Hispano* 2:1 (1882) 8–14.

Cornell, Deirdre. *Jesus Was a Migrant*. Maryknoll, NY: Orbis, 2014.

Cruz, Gemma T. *Toward a Theology of Migration: Social Justice and Religious Experience*. New York: Palgrave Macmillan, 2014.

De La Torre, Miguel A. *The U.S. Immigration Crisis: Toward an Ethics of Place.* Eugene, OR: Cascade, 2016.

Dinan, Stephen. "'Public Charge' Rule Linking Welfare Use to Green Card Chances Take Effect." *The Washington Times,* February 24, 2020. https://www.washingtontimes.com/news/2020/feb/24/public-charge-rule-linking-welfare-use-to-green-ca.

———. "Trump Enforces 'Public Charge' Rule Linking Immigrant Welfare Use to Green Card Chances." *The Washington Times,* February 24, 2020. https://www.washingtontimes.com/news/2020/feb/.

Ely, Richard T. *Social Aspects of Christianity and Other Essays.* New York: Crowell, 1889.

Esposito, Roberto. *Communitas: The Origin and Destiny of Community.* Cultural Memory in the Present. Stanford, CA: Stanford University Press, 2010.

Evans, Christopher H. "The Social Gospel as Pastoral Ministry: The Example of Ernest Fremont Tittle." *Methodist History* 35:3 (1997) 135–47.

———. *The Social Gospel in American Religion: A History.* New York: NYU Press, 2017.

Firth, David G. *Including the Stranger: Foreigners in the Former Prophets.* Downers Grove, IL: Inter Vasity, 2019.

Fosdick, Emerson. *The Hope of the World.* New York: Harper, 1933.

Francois, Willie D. "Green Cards Only for Immigrants with 'Green'?" *The Hill,* August 31, 2019. https://thehill.com/opinion/immigration/459233-green-cards-only-for-immigrants-with-green.

Gilbert, Marlea. "Hospitality in Sacred Space." *Liturgy (Washington)* 25:1 (October 22, 2009) 21–29.

Gladden, Washington. "Labor and Capital." In *The Social Gospel in America.* New York: Oxford University Press, 1966.

Goheen, Michael W. *Reading the Bible Missionally.* Grand Rapids: Eerdmans, 2016.

Gonzalez, Justo. "The Apostles' Creed and the Sanctuary Movement." *Apuntes Reflexiones Teologicas Des de El Margen Hispano* 6:1 (1986) 12–20.

———. "Sanctuary: Historical, Legal, and Biblical Considerations." *Apuntes Reflexiones Teologicas Des de El Margen Hispano* 5:2 (1985) 36–47.

Gornik, Mark R., Maria Liu Wong, Peter and Miriam Yvette Acevedo, and Timothy Keller. *Stay in the City: How Christian Faith Is Flourishing in an Urban World.* Grand Rapids: Eerdmans, 2017.

Gratton, Lynda. "The Future of Work." Lecture at the London Business School, March 29, 2017. Video recording. http://bit.ly/2fQAmop.

Heifetz, Ronald A. *The Practice of Adaptive Leadership: Tools and Tactics for Changing Your Organization and the World.* Boston: Harvard Business Press, 2009.

"In-State Tuition and State Residency Requirements." https://www.finaid.org/otheraid/stateresidency.phtml.

Lambert, Frank. *The Founding Fathers and the Place of Religion in America.* Princeton, NJ: Princeton University Press, 2010.

Madan, Monique O. "Coronavirus Testing Won't Count against Immigrants Trying to Get Green Cards, Feds Say." *Miami Herald*, March 14, 2020, https://www.miamiherald.com/news/local/immigration/.

Martin, Ley Roy. "Old Testament Foundations for Christian Hospitality." *Verbum et Ecclesia* 35:1 (2014) 1–9.

Massey M., Roter D. L. "Assessment of Immigrant Certified Nursing Assistants' Communication When Responding to Standardized Care Challenges." *Patient Education and Counseling* 99:1 (January 2016) 44–50.

Merida, Tony. "4 Practical Ways to Show Christian Hospitality." *Lifeway* (blog), January 1, 2014. https://www.lifeway.com/en/articles/practical-ways-to-show-christian-hospitality-tony-merida-ordinary.

Migration Policy Institute. "The Ethiopian Diaspora in the United States." July 2014. https://www.migrationpolicy.org/sites/default/files/publications/RAD-Ethiopia.pdf.

———. The Nigerian Diaspora in the United States." June 2015. https://www.migrationpolicy.org/sites/default/files/publications/RAD-Nigeria.pdf

Nancy, Jean-Luc, Peter Connor, and Christopher Fynsk. *The Inoperative Community*. Minneapolis: University of Minnesota Press, 1991.

Nouwen, Henri J. M. *Compassion: A Reflection on the Christian Life*. Rev. ed. New York: Image/Doubleday, 2005.

"On May 03, 1913: California Law Prohibits Asian Immigrants from Owning Land." Equal Justice Initiative. https://calender.eji.org. http://calender.eji.org/racial-injustice/may/3.

"Profile of the Unauthorized Population—MA." Migration Policy Institute. https://www.migrationpolicy.org/data/unauthorized-immigrant-population/state/MA.

"Profile of the Unauthorized Population—RI." Migration Policy Institute. https://www.migrationpolicy.org/data/unauthorized-immigrant-population/state/RI.

Quinn, Robert. *Deep Change: Discovering the Leader Within*. San Francisco: Jossey-Bass, 1996.

Rabey, Steve. "Church without Walls." *Christianity Today*, October 26, 1992.

Rauschenbusch, Walter. "Christianizing the Social Order." In *Walter Rauschenbusch: Selected Writings*, edited by Winthrops S. Hudson,166–69. New York: Paulist, 1984.

———. "The New Evangelism." In *Walter Rauschenbusch: Selected Writings*, edited by Winthrops S. Hudson, 137–65. New York: Paulist, 1984.

Reaves, Jayme R. *Safeguarding the Stranger: An Abrahamic Theology and Ethic of Protective Hospitality*. Eugene, OR: Pickwick, 2016.

Russell, Letty. *Just Hospitality: God's Welcome in World of Difference*. Louisville: Westminster John Knox, 2009.

"Sanctuary Movement." *Religion & Ethics News Weekly*, PBS, February 3, 2017. https://www.pbs.org/wnet/religionandethics/2017/02/03/sanctuary-movement/34422/.

Schott, Nils F. "Love and Stick: The Worldly Aspects of the Call in the First Letter to the Corinthians." *In Paul and the Philosophers*, edited by De Vries Hent, Blanton Ward, 310–26. New York: Fordham University Press, 2013.

Sheldon, Charles M. "The Crucifixion of Philip Strong: Chapter I Chapter II." *Maine Farmer*, February 22, 1900. American Periodicals Series 2.

———. *In His Steps*. New York: Christian Herald Bible House, 1920.

Sherman, Amy. *Restorers of Hope: Reaching the Poor in Your Community with Church-Based Ministries That Work*. Eugene, OR: Wipf & Stock, 2004.

Silbiger, Steven. *The Jewish Phenomenon: 7 Keys to the Enduring Wealth of a People*. Lanham, MD: M. Evans, 2009.

Sloane, Philip D., Christianna S. William, and Sheryl Zimmermans. "Immigrant Status and Intention to Leave of Nursing Assisitants in U.S. Nursing Homes." *Journal of American Geriatrics Society* 58:4 (2010) 731–37.

Smith, Gerald B., ed. *A Dictionary of Religion and Ethics*. New York: Macmillan, 1921.

Sutherland, Arthur. *I Was a Stranger: A Christian Theology of Hospitality*. Nashville, TN: Abingdon-Cokesbury Press, 2006.

"Undocumented Student Tuition: Overview." National Conference of State Legislatures, May 5, 2014. https://www.ncsl.org/research/education/undocumented-student-tuition-overview.aspx.

"US Travel Ban: Trump Restricts Immigration from Nigeria and Five Other Countries," *BBC* (blog), January 31, 2020, https://www.bbc.com/news/wolrd-us-canada-51335011

Thurman, Howard. *Jesus and the Disinherited*. New York: Abingdon-Cokesbury Press, 1949.

Viola, Frank. *Reimaging Church: Pursuing the Dream of Organic Christianity*. Colorado Springs, CO: David C. Cook, 2008.

Walls, Andrew F. "A Theology of Migration?." In *Crossing Cultural Frontiers: Studies in the History of World Christianity*, edited by Mark R. Gornik. Maryknoll, NY: Orbis, 2017.

"Welcoming the Stranger: A Christian Activist Responds to Trump's Immigration Order," *NC Policy Watch* (blog), February 13, 2017, http://www.ncpolicywatch.com/2017/02/13/welcoming-stranger-christian-activist-responds-trumps-immigration-.

Wells, Samuel. *A Nazareth Manifesto: Being with God*. Bognor Regis, UK: John Wiley & Sons Ltd., 2015.

———. *Incarnational Mission: Being with the World*. Grand Rapids, MI: William B. Eerdmans Publishing Company, 2018.

Index

Abraham, 86, 87–88, 98–99, 130–31
accountability, of Jeshrun
    Immigration Ministry
    (JJIM), 121–22
adaptive leadership theory, 109–10,
    122–24
advocacy, 100, 123
African churches, 13, 61–62, 134
African immigrants
    cultural diversity of, 14
    current state of, 130
    demographics of, 15
    diversity of, 129
    fate of, 17–31
    rise of, 13–17
    statistics regarding, 13–14
    vocation of, 128–34
    See also undocumented African
        immigrants (uDAIs)
Alien Land Law, 8
aloneness, 91
American dream, 26
American Immigration Lawyers
    Association, 121
Anderson, Leith, 33n1
Anderson, Mary, 82
angels, 86, 94

Anglican Church of Nativity
    Immigration Ministry
    (ACNIM), xi
Anglican Diocese of the Trinity
    (ADOTT), 15–16, 16n33
anti-immigration activists, 12
Artaxerxesin (King), 131
Arthur, John, 14–15
Asians, 8

Barnabas, 94
Bergquist, Linda, 4
Biden, Joe, 16, 78
brain drain, 130

capital, 42
Cephas, 94
Chavez, Marta, 8
Christianizing the Social Order
    (Rauschenbusch), 41
Christians, hospitality of, 82, 93–104
church
    as adviser to immigrants, 25
    as community, 78–79
    cultural shifts for, 34–36
    as edifices, 48n6
    hospitality in, 104–6